MW01146450

"After growing up in the church, I deconstructed Christianity as the _____ apparatus of my youth group was removed and questions I'd never dealt with began to bear down on my fragile faith. I wish I'd had Ian Harber's *Walking Through Deconstruction* then, but I am immensely grateful that we have it now. With both compassion and conviction, equal parts comfort and confrontation, this book will help those deconstructing see a path toward reconstruction, guiding us toward a faith more rich, robust, and dynamic in discipleship to Jesus."

Jay Y. Kim, lead pastor of WestGate Church and author of *Analog Christian*

"Ian Harber neither valorizes deconstruction nor dismisses this painful experience. As a result, he has written a book that can help anyone undergoing this process as well as everyone who loves them. *Walking Through Deconstruction* deserves a wide audience and careful reading."

Collin Hansen, vice president for content at The Gospel Coalition and author of *Timothy Keller: His Intellectual and Spiritual Formation*

"I picked up this book in hope of finding a resource to help me walk alongside those who are deconstructing. I found not only that, but also a powerful reminder of why the Christian faith drew my own heart back from the brink of unbelief. What a gift!"

Amanda Held Opelt, speaker, songwriter, and author of *A Hole in the World*

"For too long we've treated deconstruction as an intellectual problem. We think that if we can correct someone's bad ideas, then we can argue them back into the faith. But people aren't brains on sticks, they're people. Each has a story, emotions, hurts, joys, and unfathomable complexity. Ian Harber's *Walking Through Deconstruction* is the first book I've encountered that cuts to the heart of deconstruction: a painful, confusing, heartbreaking crisis of faith. And Harber goes one step further, gently walking readers through the process of reconstruction. Not with modernist apologetics but with ancient wisdom—the very beauty that pulled him out of his own crisis. Whether you're deconstructing or someone you love is, *Walking Through Deconstruction* is a generous, hopeful invitation back to Jesus."

Patrick K. Miller, pastor and director of digital relationships at The Crossing in Columbia, Missouri

"The conversation around deconstruction has too often turned into an abstract online battleground. Ian Harber reminds us of what deconstruction is actually about: the people going through it. Wise, measured, and thoughtful, this is a book that meets this moment with grace and hope."

Kaitlyn Schiess, author of *The Liturgy of Politics* and *The Ballot and the Bible*

"Having gone through it himself, Ian Harber is well positioned to tackle the delicate topic of faith deconstruction in a way that is both loving and truth telling. This book will make those in the deconstruction process feel seen but also challenged. And it will help loved ones be better equipped to walk with the deconstructing in compassionate and constructive ways."

Brett McCracken, senior editor at The Gospel Coalition and author of *The Wisdom Pyramid: Feeding Your Soul in a Post-Truth World*

WALKING THROUGH DECONSTRUCTION

*HOW TO BE A COMPANION
IN A CRISIS OF FAITH*

IAN HARBER

FOREWORD BY *GAVIN ORTLUND*

An imprint of InterVarsity Press
Downers Grove, Illinois

InterVarsity Press
P.O. Box 1400 | Downers Grove, IL 60515-1426
ivpress.com | email@ivpress.com

InterVarsity Press® is the publishing division of InterVarsity Christian Fellowship/USA®. For more information, visit intervarsity.org.

Scripture quotations, unless otherwise noted, have been taken from the Christian Standard Bible®. Copyright © 2017 by Holman Bible Publishers. Used by permission. Christian Standard Bible® and CSB® are federally registered trademarks of Holman Bible Publishers.

While any stories in this book are true, some names and identifying information may have been changed to protect the privacy of individuals.

The publisher cannot verify the accuracy or functionality of website URLs used in this book beyond the date of publication.

Cover design: David Fassett
Interior design: Jeanna Wiggins
Images: Moment / Getty Images: © Xuanyu Han, © DiggPirate, © Eugene Mymrin, © lingqi xie, © Akaradech Pramoonsin; iStock / Getty Images Plus: © francescoch

ISBN 978-1-5140-0856-0 (print) | ISBN 978-1-5140-0857-7 (digital)

Printed in the United States of America ♾

Library of Congress Cataloging-in-Publication Data
Names: Harber, Ian, 1993- author.
Title: Walking through deconstruction : how to be a companion in a crisis of faith / Ian Harber.
Description: Downers Grove, IL : IVP, [2025] | Includes bibliographical references.
Identifiers: LCCN 2024031175 (print) | LCCN 2024031176 (ebook) | ISBN 9781514008560 (print) | ISBN 9781514008577 (digital)
Subjects: LCSH: Belief and doubt–Religious aspects–Christianity. | Deconstruction. | Spiritual life. | BISAC: RELIGION / Christian Ministry / Adult
Classification: LCC BT774 .H34 2025 (print) | LCC BT774 (ebook) | DDC 231/.042–dc23/eng/20240801
LC record available at https://lccn.loc.gov/2024031175
LC ebook record available at https://lccn.loc.gov/2024031176

32   31   30   29   28   27   26   25 | 12   11   10   9   8   7   6   5   4   3   2   1

CONTENTS

FOREWORD

Gavin Ortlund

We are currently living through the greatest season of religious decline in the history of the United States. About 40 million people have stopped going to church, many of whom also no longer make any profession of Christianity. The percentage of religious "nones" (those who have no profession of any religion) has risen to roughly one-third of the population. According to many predictions, the percentage of Christians will plunge to less than half the population by 2070.[1]

My guess is that most of you reading this book don't need to be convinced of the urgency of this crisis. For many of us, these are not just statistics. This topic is personal. We see it all around us, on social media, and in the news. We have friends, family, and coworkers who have deconstructed their faith, or are currently doing so. Perhaps you yourself are going through that right now!

The word *deconstruction* can be used in different ways, and even attempting to define the term gets controversial. But no one can deny that deconstruction has different results for different people. For some, it ultimately results in a stronger faith. For others, it has an opposite effect—often involving a departure from the faith. In almost all cases, it is a painful and confusing process. What is

abundantly clear is that there is an urgent need for pastoral, coura-
geous, wise, reasoned responses, to help those who are struggling
and seeking answers.

If you want to be better equipped to respond to the deconstruction
movement—whether because of your own experience, someone you
love's experience, or the church at large—this book will be invaluable
to you. Ian Harber understands deconstruction from the inside out.
He has personally been through it, and he understands what it feels
like both to deconstruct your faith as well as to reconstruct it. He
knows the questions people are asking, the hurts that are often felt,
and what is *not* helpful to say.

Harber has in mind specifically those who have left the church
because of negative experiences. He is writing to help the church
know how to respond in such circumstances. If you are a pastor, a
parent, a friend, or an onlooker, let him be your guide. As he shows
us, the goal is not having the right answers, but a whole posture that
is above all rooted in *love*—love for neighbor, and love for Christ and
his truth.

In this book Harber walks us through the process of deconstruction
—its causes, what it feels like, and how it relates to broader trends in
the church and culture. Then he helps us understand the process of
reconstruction. Of course, we cannot control reconstruction. It is the
work of God—in us and in others. But we can understand how God
works through our suffering, through our questions. And we can grow
to create cultures and environments that help people along the way.
Ultimately, what we all need is Jesus himself. That is where Harber
points us.

For those who don't understand why deconstruction is a thing, this
book will help sensitize and inform. Many of us don't take deconstruction seriously enough. We don't understand the depth of the
problems that are fueling it. We need Harber's brutal honesty. We
need to *listen* better. We need more humility, more openheartedness.
People going through deconstruction are in *crisis*, and glib reactions

can damage them deeply. Harber shows us why careful listening is a crucial part of responding to deconstruction.

But for those who are struggling and don't see a light at the end of the tunnel, this book also points to hope. *There is hope* on the other side of deconstruction. Harber shows us how to actually help people, and what practical steps we should take when we ourselves are struggling with the intense pain of deconstruction. He highlights the importance of being "a non-anxious presence," and not needing to have all the answers—without discounting the importance of orthodoxy. He helps us understand the kinds of spaces we need to create in our churches for effective discipleship. Ultimately, he directs us to look to the Lord himself.

I would love to give a copy of this book to everyone in the church today. What Harber proposes is what we need to navigate the deconstruction crisis. His counsel will help us serve those around us who are struggling. And it will direct us all to Christ himself, the wise and good Risen King, who can bear all our doubts and burdens, and who will ultimately lead us safely through every dark night of the soul into the glorious light of heaven.

INTRODUCTION

Raised in the church, I was always in trouble. But I wasn't in trouble because of my behavior. In fact, I was mostly well-behaved when all was said and done. No, it was my *questions* that always found me trouble.

I followed the rules in the conservative evangelical church I grew up attending and tried to live a godly life as best as I knew how. But as I grew and encountered new ideas and perspectives, I began to question my beliefs. I grappled with issues like the concept of hell, the treatment of women and immigrants in the church, the problem of evil, science, and more. Ultimately, I found that my faith couldn't provide the answers I was seeking.

So, I left my faith as I knew it behind. The voices I discovered spoke of faith in an open and inclusive manner, or so it seemed to me. They embraced science, supported those marginalized by society, and believed that, in the end, everyone is saved. My media consumption spurred my deconstruction. I listened to podcasts like *The Liturgists* and watched countless hours of talks from Pete Rollins, Rob Bell, Richard Rohr, and many more. I all but dropped out of church and replaced my pastors with podcasters. I stopped trusting those who knew me in real life—my struggles, my propensities, my sorrows—and only trusted those who delivered spiritual goods to me in the form of MP3s and WAV files.

I still identified as a Christian for most of my deconstruction, talked about Jesus and the Bible, and even worked in ministry for a while. Still, my beliefs were no longer recognizably Christian. Jesus wasn't the only path. He didn't physically rise from the dead. There was no call for personal salvation. The Bible didn't hold authority in the way I had once believed. I deconstructed my faith until almost nothing substantive remained.

I wonder if this story resonates with you. Do you know someone with a similar journey? Or maybe you can relate to it yourself? This narrative of deconstruction is becoming increasingly prevalent among those raised in the church. The term *deconstruction* has gained traction in recent years and seems to be everywhere now. It's causing rifts in churches, families, and friendships, as individuals who once shared a faith now find themselves divided. Some remain steadfast in their beliefs, while others, like me, unravel their faith due to doubts, questions, and critical concerns.

Let me share a few more parts of my story. Though I grew up in a loving home, I was raised by my grandparents. My father abandoned me as a toddler, and my mother struggled with addiction her whole life. My grandparents were incredible, but my grandmother was diagnosed with cancer when I was young and passed away the day after Christmas when I was thirteen. A few years later, my mother took her own life. Between those two funerals, I attended ten others for various other friends and family members. Fast-forward to the year after my wedding, when my grandfather passed away in a plane crash accident. Death has been on my doorstep my entire life.

In my youth group, a mentor who had laid the foundation of my faith and even baptized me went on to sexually abuse multiple friends of mine. Despite having a compassionate youth pastor (not the same person who abused my friends), the church I attended was rigid, legalistic, and often promoted partisan politics from the pulpit. The Christian school I went to ostracized me for asking questions, wrestling with my faith, and trying to figure things out. Another church

I was a part of caused tremendous pain in my life through betrayal and rejection.

Given all this, can you fault me for having questions? For feeling that the church couldn't address my deepest needs? Even if my journey led me to unhelpful places, it's understandable why I sought anything I could find to make sense of the pain I endured. After a tumultuous upbringing and attending churches with their own sets of challenges, I deconstructed my faith. For many years, my faith was barely hanging on.

It took nearly a decade, but eventually my faith reconstructed. It was through seeking out a theological education in another local church, where my questions were accepted, the Bible was opened, the riches of church history were taught, and genuine discipleship was modeled, and through the grace of God—which met me in a dark season of my life—that I was able to find a foundation for my faith. It was through landing at a church with people who genuinely cared, after experiencing significant pain from a church I had trusted, that I learned the importance of the local church.

Today, my faith is stronger than ever. I don't have all the answers, but I've gained something even better: a *settled trust in the Lord*. I stand as evidence that walking through deconstruction can lead to a more robust, renewed faith. But that's not the outcome for everyone.

A few years back, I shared my journey of deconstruction and reconstruction in an article for The Gospel Coalition.[1] The response—both support and criticism—was overwhelming. Many related to my story, while others felt threatened by its honesty or by the fact that despite years of deconstruction, I'm still a Christian who adheres to the historic orthodox tradition.[2] This made me reflect not just on my own journey but on the process of deconstruction as a whole. As I pondered my experience and the discussions surrounding deconstruction, I realized that many people were touching on various facets of it but missing the bigger picture.

The term *deconstruction* has come to have many meanings, leading to lots of confusion about what it is and isn't. It's become a word with a negative connotation because its definition is so ambiguous. I believe we need clarity, not to confine anyone or gatekeep an experience, but to understand and minister to those truly going through it. Lots of books are being written about deconstruction right now. Most of the books I have seen have been written by pastors, professors, or writers for people who are in the process of deconstructing—and some of them are very good! We need these books to be written. But what about from the opposite direction? From someone who has deconstructed and reconstructed their faith writing *to the church* and *for the church*. Plenty of angry exvangelicals have written their tell-all memoirs railing against the failures of the church. Plenty of fundamentalists have written to warn people about the dangers of deconstruction. What I hope to do in this book is *serve* the church in this crucial ministry as someone who has been deeply hurt by the church and wonderfully healed by Jesus through the ministry of the local church.

This book could never have been written if I hadn't gone through deconstruction—but this book isn't about me. This book is about you and the people you love and minister to who are deconstructing their faith. I imagine you are coming to this book with lots of questions. What is deconstruction? What causes it? What is the experience like? How can we help people who are deconstructing? Is there anything we can do to make deconstruction less intense and prevalent in our churches? These are the topics that this book sets out to address.

WHO IS DECONSTRUCTING?

If you're reading this book, someone you know is probably deconstructing. Whether it's someone in your church, a friend, a child, a parent, a coworker, or someone else you care about, they are wrestling with their faith in a significant way that might scare you. Regardless of any statistics or trends, that person is the most important one to you.

It's easy to write something like deconstruction off as a trend that all the cool kids are doing just because it seems to be everywhere these days. Whenever you bring up deconstruction being trendy, you'll rightly receive some visceral pushback from those who are experiencing it because, to them, there is nothing trendy about it. I hope it will become clear why that is in the first few chapters of this book.

Deconstruction isn't a *trendy* thing to do, but it is a *trend* that is happening at scale in our country and passing from person to person. Anecdotally, when I look up various hashtags on TikTok, the views on deconstruction content are through the roof. As of the time of writing this book, I see 1 billion views on #deconstruction, 85.5 million views on #deconstructiontiktok, 61.2 million views on #progressivechristianity, 17.5 million views on #deconstructionjourney, 1.1 million views on #deconstructiongrief. There is nothing particularly scientific about looking up views on some hashtags on a social media platform, but what it *does* indicate is that deconstruction is in the digital air. At a minimum, people are being algorithmically served content about deconstruction all the time. They are exposed to people's deconversion stories and challenges to the faith in ways that are historically unprecedented. The algorithm isn't going to wait for your Bible study.

But thankfully, reliable quantitative research around this has brought some helpful insights to light. Jim Davis, Michael Graham, and Ryan Burge have released the largest study ever done on dechurching in America in their book *The Great Dechurching: Who's Leaving, Why Are They Going, and What Will It Take to Bring Them Back?* Forty million Americans have left the church over the last twenty-five years. It's the largest religious shift in American history—and it's *away* from the church.[3]

The reality is that not everyone who has dechurched has deconstructed—not even most of them. The authors profile five different types of people who have dechurched, and they split the five profiles into two groups: the casually dechurched and the dechurched casualties. The casually dechurched are those who left the church for casual reasons: they got too busy, they moved and never found a new church, they stopped going to church during the Covid-19 pandemic and never went back, and so on.[4] The other group, dechurched casualties, make up about ten million adult Americans who have "permanently, purposefully exited evangelicalism."[5] These are the people who have left the church because of real, negative experiences they have had in the church. My book is about the dechurched casualties.

According to the study, these dechurched casualties—who the authors call exvangelicals—are 82 percent white, 13 percent black, and 2 percent Hispanic. They're 65 percent female and 35 percent male. Maybe most surprisingly, the average age is fifty-four years old. What the study shows is that the average exvangelical is a white, Gen X female who didn't feel like they fit in with their church, didn't feel loved, found it inconvenient to attend, had negative experiences, and disagreed with the politics and beliefs of their church.[6] This may or may not describe the person you know who is deconstructing. But I would bet it describes the progressive voices they're listening to in their deconstruction journey.

There's something else to keep in mind: these people in the study are the ones who have *already* left the church and have no intention of ever coming back. They are *not* the people who are still in the church wrestling through whether they're going to remain Christian and stay in the church. We have no reason to believe the trajectory of dechurching will reverse any time soon. As people are exposed to media and peers that challenge their faith and are raised in the homes of those who have left the church, we're going to see more and more people deconstructing their faith in the years—and maybe decades—to come.

Some will point out that what we need to help people in their deconstruction is more apologetics. Apologetics can be a good thing. We need to be able to speak intelligently about our faith. But apologetics without love, without character, without personal integrity, without a gracious and compassionate heart is nothing more than a clanging cymbal (1 Corinthians 13:1-3). Having answers is good; having love is better. "What matters is faith working through love" (Galatians 5:6).

THE PATH OF DECONSTRUCTION
AND RECONSTRUCTION

In this book, I walk you through the path of deconstruction and reconstruction. Part one of the book is all about deconstruction: we define what deconstruction is and isn't, as well as what catalyzes deconstruction (chapter one); situate deconstruction in the Christian life (chapter two); describe the existential experience of deconstruction (chapter three); look at how deconstruction affects our beliefs (chapter four); see how the church plays a role in deconstruction (chapter five); identify how sin and cultural pressures create a weak sense of identity that contributes to deconstruction (chapter six); and examine the potential outcomes of deconstruction (chapter seven).

My goal isn't to make you deconstruct your faith, but to help you understand why others are deconstructing theirs. I want to warn you, though, that it is a difficult journey. You might encounter some things that offend you and other things that cause you to question. It can be a painful process, but there's no healing without first acknowledging and understanding the brokenness. Whether you feel a deep resonance or repulsion with the journey of deconstruction, I ask that you read it while keeping in mind the person you know who is deconstructing, opening your heart wide to them and asking God to help you see them in this process.

Don't worry, I won't leave you at the bottom of deconstruction. Part two of the book focuses on reconstruction. The truth is that we can't control someone's reconstruction. What we *can* do is create environments—both in our interpersonal relationships and in our churches—that help minimize the *intensity* of someone's deconstruction by being a non-anxious presence, creating healthy relationships and churches full of trust and care, and having a more robust understanding of our faith to talk through with them.

To that end, we look at how we can handle our relationships (chapter eight), how God uses our suffering (chapter nine), how we hold our beliefs (chapter ten), how we view the Christian life (chapter eleven), and how we can create healthy churches (chapter twelve). Finally, we gaze at God himself to see his goodness and beauty (chapter thirteen).

Everyone's deconstruction story is unique to them. Sure, there are commonalities and contours that many share, but you can't assume everyone who says "I'm deconstructing my faith" is doing so for the exact same reason. That makes writing a book like this a difficult task. How do you describe something that is so personal? Inevitably there will be a point where the shoe simply doesn't fit.

With that in mind, I'd like to give you a tip for reading this book. Instead of reading this book as a comprehensive explanation for every individual deconstruction story, read it more like a puzzle where each individual chapter is a piece of the puzzle. The goal is to develop a clearer picture of the person you know who is deconstructing and how to best love them and minister to them. Some pieces fit better than others. Some pieces only fit in specific places. Other pieces go with an entirely different puzzle and simply don't belong. Maybe one chapter doesn't apply at all and another chapter is a bull's-eye. Some chapters will feel more or less relevant depending on who you have in mind. What is most relevant might change over time. That's okay.

Deconstruction is a messy and complicated process. My hope is that you are equipped for all kinds of different situations at the end of this book. Our goal is to faithfully walk alongside our loved ones who are deconstructing their faith and surrender ourselves as an instrument in God's hands, praying for the renewal of their faith.

As we start on this journey, I'll make two promises to you: this book will be *brutally honest* yet *defiantly hopeful*. If you think we can ignore the problems in American evangelicalism, part one of this book will be a rude awakening. If you think I'm down and out on Jesus, the church, and living a faithful Christian life, part two of this book will surprise you with the amount of hope that I truly have.

The missionary Lesslie Newbigin is often attributed with saying, "I am neither an optimist nor a pessimist; Jesus Christ is risen from the dead!" I hope to capture that sentiment in this book. Jesus Christ has risen indeed, and nothing—no doubt, scandal, leader, church, or culture—can separate us from his love.

PART 1

DECONSTRUCT

DEFINING
DECONSTRUCTION

"I'M DECONSTRUCTING MY FAITH." Perhaps someone has said this to you recently. A friend, child, spouse, parent, coworker, or congregant. You don't really know what they mean, but it doesn't sound good. Just from the name, you can tell they are taking something apart. If it's their faith they're deconstructing, then they must be taking their faith apart. But why?

As you start asking questions, you quickly realize you've gotten yourself in over your head. They might start asking questions about the Bible, God, or the church that you've never thought about before. Or maybe you have thought about them, but they felt so big that you simply pushed them out of your mind and forgot about them. Maybe it's something you haven't thought about since seminary (if you went). They might start talking about large cultural and political issues that seem like they came out of nowhere. They begin accusing the church of doing this or not doing that. "Where is this coming from?" you wonder.

The questions and the accusations that you hear from them put you on edge. You start to feel anxiety well up inside of you. You think of the other popular deconstruction stories that you've heard of—Michael Gungor, Joshua Harris, Audrey Assad, and more, none of whom are Christians anymore. Your mind starts racing a hundred miles per hour. "Are they losing their faith?" "I thought they loved Jesus!" "I wonder if they're in some kind of sin." "I'm overwhelmed by all of these questions." And it all comes down to this one word to describe it: *deconstruction.*

The word *deconstruction* goes back to the philosopher Jacques Derrida, who used it in a technical way to describe the process of "critically reevaluat[ing] the fundamental arrangement and operations of any and all forms of analysis."[1] If that sounds confusing, that's because it is. Deconstruction, by its nature, is difficult to describe because it's a process that deconstructs the very words needed to describe it. But it's insufficient to say that deconstruction is simply a process of analysis or critique.

Here's the primary difference: in other forms of analysis or critique, there is typically a method that is followed in order to reach a predetermined outcome. Think of the scientific method. After observing a phenomenon, you ask questions about it and research existing answers or solutions. If you don't find any satisfactory answers, you pose a hypothesis, perform a set of experiments to test your hypothesis, and draw conclusions from your experiments about whether your hypothesis has been proven right or wrong.

Deconstruction isn't like this. There is no set process and no predetermined conclusion to deconstruction. It's not a process you decide to undertake to investigate a problem. It's something you encounter and enter into. The only thing you can do in deconstruction is allow the process to unfold and follow it where it goes.[2] The difference between Derrida's philosophy of deconstruction and how faith deconstruction is thought about today is that it doesn't have to last forever. Not only that, but there is precedent for what we now call deconstruction that predates Derrida. More on that later.

It's only in the last thirty years or so that *deconstruction* really began to describe a particular phenomenon within popular-level evangelical Christianity. Christians started to use the word to describe the process of reexamining their faith to reveal the contradictions in it and produce something better—at least as they perceived it to be. This became the hallmark of what would eventually be called the Emergent Church.

The Emergent Church was a movement in the early 2000s that was led by pastors and writers such as Doug Pagitt, Brian McLaren, Rob Bell, Peter Rollins, Donald Miller, Mark Driscoll, Richard Rohr, and many more. The Emergent Church started out as an ecclesial project that was searching for ways to reinvent the forms of the church for a postmodern world. But the ecclesial project morphed into a doctrinal project. Instead of simply deconstructing the current ways of doing church, they began deconstructing the core beliefs of the Christian faith. Many (not all) of the names associated with the Emergent movement have either left the faith altogether or redefined it in ways that are beyond recognition.[3]

But something different is happening today. It's related to Derrida's ideas of deconstruction, and it's certainly related to the Emergent Church movement, but there seems to be more going on under this wave of deconstruction than what either of those other two waves were attempting to get at. This latest wave of deconstruction is what this book is attempting to make sense of. What is it? What causes it? What is the experience like? And how can we—as believers who walk with those who are experiencing it, and as believers leading our churches—help them?

WHAT DECONSTRUCTION ISN'T

There are many narratives surrounding what this wave of deconstruction is and isn't. Most of these narratives are getting at parts of what is going on but miss other aspects that are crucial to it. If we want to understand what deconstruction *is*, then we might want to start by understanding what it *isn't*.

Asking questions. One popular narrative is that deconstruction is simply asking questions about your faith. One time, I was getting coffee with a new friend and shared parts of my story with him. I briefly mentioned how I went through deconstruction. After a while, he came back to it and said, "I want to talk about that. I sometimes have questions about my faith, and I was wondering: Am I deconstructing?" The idea that deconstruction is simply asking questions about your faith raises all kinds of *other* questions.

What about that time when the disciples were physically present at Jesus' ascension? Matthew records it by saying, "When they saw him, they worshiped, but some doubted" (Matthew 28:17). The eleven disciples had already witnessed three years of Jesus' ministry, his death, his burial, his miraculous, world-changing, paradigm-shifting resurrection. They had spent forty days with Jesus after his resurrection and were now watching him ascend into heaven, to the right hand of the Father, with their own eyes—and they still somehow doubted. Is *that* deconstruction?

If deconstruction is nothing more than having questions about your faith, you might as well put this book down, because *every* Christian has done that. If that's true, then there's no conversation to be had. We're all deconstructing. End of story. We might as well stop using the word entirely.

There is more going on than that. When we talk to those we know who are deconstructing or we hear the stories of people in our churches, our communities, or online who are deconstructing, we can tell that it's more than mere questions, but we may not completely grasp what is actually going on.

Deconstruction certainly isn't *less* than asking questions, but it's much *more* than that. If we stop there, then we won't have an adequate understanding of what it is and the experience of going through it. We'll fail to have a grasp of it and won't be able to minister to those who are going through it. We'll fail to create environments that lessen the intensity of people's deconstruction and fail to aid in their faith flourishing into confident trust in the risen Christ.

One step toward apostasy. The opposite extreme of the asking questions narrative is thinking deconstruction is nothing more than a brief stop on the way to apostasy. Usually, the people who think of deconstruction in this way have one goal in mind: defending the faith. They want to defend orthodox doctrine, the Bible, and the purity of the church. All of these are good things worth defending. The problem is not in these people's desire to defend the faith but in their posture. They see anyone who questions the faith at all as, at best, problems to be fixed or, at worst, enemies in need of defeat.

They're armed with the weapons of modernist apologetics and are ready to give you rational proofs for intelligent design, the reliability of the Bible, and the bodily resurrection. It's *good* to know why you believe these things and be able to articulate them. But when they are used as weapons against an enemy instead of "a reason for the hope that is in you" (1 Peter 3:15), they become instruments of division instead of testaments to God's glory. By misunderstanding the experience of deconstruction in this way, they turn sincere seekers into formidable foes to be fought in a spiritual war.

Consider this definition of deconstruction by Stand to Reason, a conservative apologetics organization. They define deconstruction this way: "The process of pulling apart undesirable aspects of your Christian faith to make them align with culture or your own personal beliefs."[4] Defining deconstruction like this assumes a lot about the *motives* of the person deconstructing. The reality is that everyone's motives are mixed and messy. It's natural to find aspects of the Christian faith undesirable on the surface because they grind against our sinful natures and cultural norms. We're being transformed through the renewing of our minds, and that process inevitably includes some growing pains. This is true for all of us who are pursuing Christ with all our hearts, not just those who are deconstructing. To say that people who are deconstructing just want to pull apart undesirable aspects of the faith is to attack them for an impulse that, if we were honest with ourselves, most of us have felt at different times in our life and in different aspects of our faith.

Not only that, this definition ignores many things that would actually lead someone to deconstruct in the first place. It individualizes deconstruction by isolating the person who is deconstructing from their broader communal and cultural context, which just isn't how faith works. No one's faith is purely individual. It's influenced by a whole host of factors that are both inside and outside the person. This definition assumes a maliciousness on the part of the person deconstructing that simply can't be assumed without further conversation.

If a person *is* deconstructing simply because they find the faith undesirable and want to conform it to their own personal beliefs, then we already have a word for that: apostasy. There isn't any struggle to keep the historic faith, only a desire to reshape it into their own image. But that isn't the full story when it comes to deconstruction. Those who are deconstructing are undergoing a far more complex and emotionally taxing process.

Here's the difference: by and large, when someone begins deconstructing, they aren't looking for a way to leave the faith; they are looking for a way to *stay* in the faith. Of course, like we just said, motives are messy. Who can know the depths of our hearts but God alone? But if someone simply wanted to leave the faith, they would. People do that all the time. They fade away over time or simply stop being Christians because they were never interested in being one in the first place. But deconstruction isn't that simple. There are other dynamics at play other than just wanting to leave Jesus behind.

Deconstruction isn't letting go of faith; it's holding on to the smallest string of faith someone can find for as long as they can. Just because some people choose to let go doesn't mean that letting go is inevitable. If we treat it as inevitable, it might turn out to be a self-fulfilling prophecy.

"Good" deconstruction versus "bad" deconstruction. There is another narrative in Christian circles surrounding deconstruction that goes something like this: There are two kinds of deconstruction—healthy deconstruction and unhealthy deconstruction. Healthy deconstruction is good. Unhealthy deconstruction is bad.

Healthy deconstruction is when you examine your faith and untangle it from the cultural ideologies that aren't actually Christian in order to have a purer faith. Even Jesus deconstructed! Remember when he said, "You have heard it said . . . but I say"?[5] Martin Luther deconstructed! Remember when he nailed the Ninety-Five Theses to the Wittenberg door? When you deconstruct using the Bible and within your church community, it can be the best thing to ever happen to your faith. Deconstruction is healthy when you do it right.[6]

Unhealthy deconstruction is when you leave the Bible and the church behind and only seek to destroy your faith. It's not deconstruction; it's demolition. You're not trying to seek God; you're only trying to seek personal freedom—and probably freedom to sin. Instead of using Scripture to examine your culture, you're using culture to examine Scripture. It's a given that you won't have faith after you've deconstructed because you never really wanted to keep your faith in the first place.

On the surface, I understand why people say this. There were a couple of years when I repeated this narrative myself. It's getting at the fact that there is a questioning and wrestling with faith that is good. It's not abnormal or bad to doubt, have questions, or seek to untangle your faith from cultural lies that have seeped in from one place or another. Wanting to commend people for seeking truth is itself commendable, and I would rather people believe this narrative than think that all doubt and questioning is bad. Unfortunately, there are too many churches and relationships where asking questions at all is looked down on.

There is truth to this way of thinking about deconstruction, but it's missing something. People don't wake up one day with the conscious thought, "I want to be closer to the Lord. I guess I should deconstruct my faith! What's the healthiest way for me to do that?"

The person who is deconstructing did not choose to deconstruct. You, the person walking with them, cannot control their process of deconstruction. Deconstruction is an experience that happens *to* you. You don't make a rational decision to deconstruct your faith. You realize you're deconstructing after it has already begun. This, as you might imagine, is a terrifying realization. The reason people who are deconstructing bristle at the idea of "good versus bad" deconstruction is that it feels as though people are trying to control them in a process that cannot be controlled.

You might be starting to understand why deconstruction can be such a difficult topic to discuss. It's difficult to know exactly what we're talking about when we talk about deconstruction. We need a working definition that captures the basic ideas of the process while being flexible enough to account for the various ways people experience deconstruction in their individual stories.

A WORKING DEFINITION OF DECONSTRUCTION

Now that we've walked through ways of thinking about deconstruction that are more or less helpful, but ultimately incomplete, is there an alternative, more encompassing way of defining it? I think there is.

However we define *deconstruction*, it needs to meet two main criteria. It needs to (1) describe a wide array of experiences that—to a greater or lesser degree—would be affirmed as accurate by someone who is deconstructing or has deconstructed and (2) be useful for people who are walking with and ministering to those who are deconstructing, so that they can better understand the experience and walk with them through it in a way that respects them and the process.

If how we define deconstruction doesn't allow both groups to talk to each other with mutual understanding, then we've failed. If, however, our definition can act as an explanatory bridge between those who are deconstructing and those who desire to minister to them, it will serve as a helpful tool for fostering a better conversation, less reactivity, and, hopefully, stronger faith.

Let's get to our working definition of deconstruction, which we will spend the rest of part one of this book unpacking. Here is how I define deconstruction: "Deconstruction is a crisis of faith that leads to the questioning of core doctrines and untangling of cultural ideologies that settles in a faith that is different from before."

You can divide the definition into four parts:

1. A crisis of faith

2. Questioning of core doctrines

3. Untangling of cultural ideologies

4. Settling in a faith that is different from before

Each of the four parts of the definition is crucial to understanding what deconstruction is, but the most important part about this definition is that deconstruction is, before anything else, a *crisis of faith*. We can talk about doctrine, culture, and reconstruction all we want. Still, if we do not acknowledge that deconstruction is first and foremost a crisis of faith, then we have not understood deconstruction. Chapters two and three are dedicated to understanding the crisis.

DIFFERENT KINDS OF DECONSTRUCTION

If you talk to more than one person about their deconstruction, you'll quickly realize that not everyone's deconstruction story is the same. That's why trying to define it is risky business. The moment you define it is the moment someone says, "That's not me!" So, a working definition of deconstruction is only as helpful as it is flexible.

Someone might experience more of a cultural deconstruction, while another might have more of a doctrinal deconstruction. A cultural deconstruction could lead to a doctrinal deconstruction and vice versa. Two different people might have the same questions and concerns but experience them at different levels of intensity. One might feel like their whole world is falling apart, and another might be bothered but not perceive it as much of a threat.

Think about this definition like a chart that you can plot points on. On the x-axis you have cultural on one side and doctrinal on the other. On the y-axis you have high intensity at the top and low intensity at the bottom. Someone's experience of deconstruction can be plotted at any point on the chart, and it can move over time. Just because someone starts out at one point doesn't mean they will stay there. A relatively low-intensity cultural deconstruction can result in a high-intensity doctrinal deconstruction and vice versa.

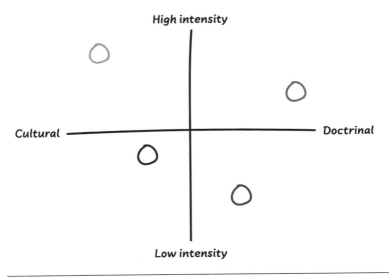

Figure 1.1. A working definition of deconstruction as plotted on an x-y chart

In the introduction, I mentioned treating this book like a puzzle with different pieces depending on the person who is deconstructing. This is one way to start thinking of deconstruction in dynamic terms rather than as a single, monolithic experience. Deconstruction is messy, complicated, and deeply personal. How we think about it must be flexible enough to understand a whole host of different experiences.

Now that we have a working definition of what deconstruction *is*, let's briefly look at what the experience of deconstruction is *like*.

TESTING BY FIRE

There's a passage of Scripture that has become ground zero in my understanding of deconstruction. It captures many key components of the experience so well and succinctly that it serves as a helpful starting point. In 1 Corinthians 3:11-15, Paul gives us the clearest description of deconstruction in the Bible. He says,

> For no one can lay any foundation other than what has been laid down. That foundation is Jesus Christ. If anyone builds on the foundation with gold, silver, costly stones, wood, hay, or straw, each one's work will become obvious. For the day will disclose it, because it will be revealed by fire; the fire will test the quality of each one's work. If anyone's work that he has built survives, he will receive a reward. If anyone's work is burned up, he will experience loss, but he himself will be saved—but only as through fire.[7]

There are at least four takeaways from this passage that are relevant to our thinking about deconstruction:

1. Christianity falls apart without the foundation of Jesus Christ himself.
2. The quality of materials that make up a house of faith varies. "Gold, silver, [and] costly stones" are good materials that aren't easily affected by fires; in fact, they're *refined* by fire. "Wood, hay, or straw" are bad materials that are easily destroyed by fire.
3. There will be a day when the quality of everyone's materials that make up their house of faith will be tested through fire.
4. The experience of going through this fire will be felt as "experienc[ing] loss." This means it won't simply be an intellectual exercise, but it will involve a grieving process.

These four points mean that the various beliefs we hold in our faith are not created equal. Some are stronger, some are weaker. And we will all, at one point or another, go through trials that will set our beliefs on fire. The beliefs built on Christ will survive. The beliefs that aren't will burn up. We will experience the burning of our beliefs as a loss, which produces a crisis, and from the crisis, grief. Until the trial is over, we won't know which beliefs will survive and which beliefs will be burned up.

WHAT LIGHTS THE FIRE?

If deconstruction is first and foremost a crisis of faith, then it's worth asking: What are the catalysts that can lead someone to experience that trapdoor opening under their faith and leaving them lost in the dark? I would like to briefly contend that there are three broad categories that act as the match that lights the fire in someone's house of faith. We explore each of these in more detail throughout the book.[8]

1. Cultural Christianity—a generation of Christians who opted for religious entertainment and moralistic therapeutic deism over devotion and discipleship, which leads to a weak foundation of faith

2. Compromised churches—a generation of churches that chose partisan politics and their reputations over spiritual formation and shepherding the flock, which leads to performative churches that have lost the plot of God's story and their purpose in it

3. Compounded anxiety—a generation of Christians who grew up experiencing hardships while having high unmet expectations for life, which led to difficulty persevering in suffering[9]

Each of these issues builds on the other. Because cultural Christianity has traded shepherds for celebrities and CEOs, the people who are supposed to care for our souls are too busy being famous or running leadership workshops to pastor their congregation. Because many of our churches have become nothing more than venues for religious entertainment instead of places to cast our cares on Jesus together, we're left in the ocean of our own anxieties to sink or swim, and, understandably, many feel like they can no longer keep swimming. Something *has* to change.

That's the hope of this book. By closely examining the fires that test people's faith, we can foster a vision of discipleship to Jesus, the strength of our relationships, and the health of our churches to help people withstand the fiery trials of life—whether they be doubts, scandals, or sufferings—and develop a thriving faith in the process.

Yet, for many with thin and low-trust relationships, no theology of suffering, no robust doctrine, no vision for discipleship, and no healthy churches they can trust, their anxieties accumulate with no resources to relieve them. The center cannot hold, and the house collapses. Our weak house has given way, and now our faith is collapsing.

Now, we're in a crisis of faith.

DECONSTRUCTING THE WALL

A CRISIS OF FAITH

My friend Jenny was telling me about how she was struggling with her faith and how no one really seemed to understand what she was experiencing. She apologized for crying.

She had talked with a friend of hers about her questions and wondered out loud if she was deconstructing. Her friend responded, with the best intentions, that deconstructing is a great thing to do because it's just critical thinking and that there was nothing to worry about because critical thinking is good. She said that every Christian should deconstruct!

Of course, critical thinking is good. To be sure, Jenny was thinking critically about her faith. She was asking questions about the authority and trustworthiness of the Bible. She was asking questions about the church's treatment of women and their role in ministry. She was questioning whether God even exists or if this whole thing we call Christianity is just a sham. Had she believed all this stuff just because those in authority told her to? How could she be sure any of this was real? Belief always felt so easy until she became a mom, and the realization set in that now she was the authority figure in her daughter's life, and she had to teach her daughter *something*. But the weight of that responsibility seemed crushing when she didn't even know if she could trust her own beliefs.

She was thinking critically, all right. But it was more than that. She couldn't sleep at night. The doubts and fear constantly occupied her mind. The question, "What if I'm wrong?" haunted her. Calling it "critical thinking" was true in one sense, and in another sense, it completely misunderstood what she was going through. It was true on a pragmatic level, but it minimized the confusion, disorientation, and, frankly, *terror*, that she felt on an experiential level. Jenny wasn't just thinking critically. She was experiencing a crisis of faith.

But Jenny's questioning of Christianity wasn't her trying to find loopholes so she could indulge in sin. Nor was she simply looking for a way to leave the faith because she was tired of being in it. She didn't want to leave the faith. She wanted to stay. She wasn't one step away from apostasy. She was desperately trying to trust Jesus and hold on in the midst of the deep questions and the dark night of the soul that she experienced.

For a long time, Jenny thought she might be a bad person—a bad *Christian*—for having those questions, but she couldn't stuff them down any longer. She had to ask them. She had never thought of deconstruction as a crisis of faith before. But when she did, it was like a lightbulb was turned on in a room that had been dark for ages. She didn't immediately have relief from the fear or answers to her questions, but she finally had language for what she was experiencing.

Jenny isn't bad for asking questions. This crisis wasn't something she sought out just because she was curious or wanted to sin or leave the faith. It's something that came to her that she had to somehow find a way to move through. It wasn't just a cold, intellectual exercise that she had to approach like a scientist or academic, testing out different hypotheses until a result was achieved. It was a grieving process. She was mourning the loss of the innocence of her faith, the trust she thought she had, and the difficult journey that lay ahead of her.

Jenny's story isn't unique. In fact, I believe that this is the story of the majority of people who would say they are deconstructing. Stories like Jenny's are exactly why I define deconstruction the way I do.

It's not enough to simply look at the *act* of deconstruction. We also need to take into account the *experience* of deconstruction. Any attempt to address one without the other will fall short, because it's only seeing part of the picture. We'll spend a significant amount of time looking at the act of deconstruction, examining the doctrines and cultural narratives that are being deconstructed. But if we don't start by understanding deconstruction as a crisis of faith before anything else, then we won't understand it at all.

IT'S NOT BACKSLIDING

You might remember people talking about "backsliding" in the '90s and '00s. When I first started deconstructing, *backsliding* was the only word I had for it. I felt so much shame for not being "on fire for God" the way I once was. The pressure in that era of evangelical subculture to always be "passionate," "on fire," and "radical" made it seem like the totality of the Christian life existed as a lifelong spiritual upward trajectory.

Conferences were created to stoke our passion for Jesus, but there were few guides that taught us how to participate in the Passion of Christ. Middle-class upward mobility was mapped onto spiritual growth as the only legitimate spiritual life. There were only three categories: growing, stagnant, or backsliding. If you talked to most kids in a youth group, they would all probably confess to some level of stagnation. They weren't reading their Bible as much as they should, praying as much as they wanted to, showing up to church each week, or something else to that effect.

There were always a few kids that leaders identified as those who were on fire and growing. Often, it was charisma being mistaken for spiritual maturity (but that's not just in youth groups, is it?). I'll never forget one time in a service, one of the leaders started calling out specific students by name to stand up in front of everyone. He publicly declared these particular students as those who were truly following Christ, and the rest of us needed to look up to and follow their example. Many of us were baffled by some of the names called. We knew what was really going on in their lives outside of class. Our leaders were fooled into thinking that the who's who of cool kids were also the most spiritually mature. It was never the quiet, the unseen, the doubting, or the questioning who were seen as mature. Those people were put in the last category: the backsliding.

The backsliding were those who had questions. They were the ones who didn't accept taught dogma at face value, the ones who wanted to wrestle with the hard topics and understand them for themselves. Because there was no category for doubt, questioning, grief, and wrestling with your faith, these people would often self-identify as backsliding because that's the only thing they thought it could be.

If you didn't *feel* God in a few weeks, you must be backsliding. You were backsliding if you had questions about the Bible because you couldn't *just believe.* If you were tempted to sin, you were backsliding because you didn't have enough faith to avoid it. It was better to be stagnant than backsliding because at least you weren't "falling away."

But these three categories—growing, stagnant, and backsliding—are new ways of thinking about the Christian life. These assume that the only legitimate spiritual life is the upwardly mobile one. We were taught to have an upper-middle-class faith that worked hard to avoid spiritual poverty—even though Jesus said those are the blessed ones (Matthew 5:3)—and to live as if we had spiritual riches. The reality is that no part of our life works like this. If we expect any aspect of life to consistently be up and to the right, we are setting ourselves up for inevitable disappointment.

C. S. Lewis understood this and wrote about what he called the Law of Undulation.[1] Life is a series of peaks and troughs through which we are constantly moving. One season of life, you're on the mountaintop; the next season of life, you're in the valley. Those seasons might be weeks, months, or years, but eventually, a peak will give way to a valley, and the valley will take you to a peak.

Lewis writes about this in his classic book *The Screwtape Letters*, a series of fictional letters from a high-ranking demon, Screwtape, to his lower-level nephew demon, Wormwood, about how to tempt a Christian. Screwtape tells Wormwood that these peaks and troughs are a normal part of life and are not in and of themselves bad, but the troughs provide ample opportunity for temptation. There is more than one way to tempt someone in a spiritual trough, Screwtape tells Wormwood, but Screwtape has a particular idea in mind. He says,

> There is an even better way of exploiting a trough; I mean through the patient's own thoughts about it. As always, the first step is to keep knowledge out of his mind. Do not let him suspect the law of undulation. Let him assume that the first ardours of his conversion might have been expected to last, and ought to have lasted, forever, and that his present dryness is an equally permanent condition.[2]

By perpetuating an up-and-to-the-right spirituality, evangelicalism has kept the Law of Undulation out of our minds and made us think that our initial spiritual fervor was going to last forever. And in seasons where the emotions and the confidence feel far from us, we similarly think that dryness will last forever as well. This simply isn't true. We are a people who are perpetually in process, and the undulation of life is an inescapable aspect of our humanity.

Giving up in a trough is the easy way out. Asking questions, wrestling, and fighting to find God in the midst of it, trusting his promise that he is with you in the valley and that goodness and mercy will follow you all the days of your life, that one day another peak may come—that is an exercise of *faith*.

My friend Jenny isn't backsliding. She is pressing into her faith more than she ever has before. By hanging on the way she is, she is exercising her faith. Saying that she is backsliding would be to completely discount the fear and grief that she is feeling while trying to hold on to her faith. She might be in a trough, but she is no farther from the Lord's reach than she was at her last peak.

HITTING "THE WALL"

If you approach the life of faith with the up-and-to-the-right framework, thinking you should always be experiencing more and more of the presence of God in your life, then it will come as a shock to you when, in a trough, you hit what some have called "The Wall." For most people who hit The Wall, it comes as a terrifying shock to the system that breaks down the categories you previously thought to be impervious. The truth, however, is that many people hit The Wall at some point in their lives, but they were never told that The Wall exists. So they either abandon their faith altogether or stuff down their fears and try to forget about it, leaving them stuck standing in front of The Wall and refusing to go through it.

Instead of an always up-and-to-the-right faith as I described above, in the book *The Critical Journey*, spiritual director Janet O. Hagberg and New Testament professor Robert A. Guelich describe six stages in the journey of someone's life of faith.

The first three stages are ones that would be recognizable to most people who have been Christians for a while: (1) awe and reverence before God with an eagerness to learn and insecurity about not knowing more, (2) a strong sense of belonging to a church community and finding a strong sense of safety and purpose by identifying with the group, and (3) feeling empowered to use your gifts in the community to productively help and serve others.

These are stages of growth that many of us can identify with. Our churches are usually set up for these kinds of people. This is the typical pathway of discipleship for most churches and is what is *right* about the up-and-to-the-right way of thinking. We want this sort of growth for people. The problem is that this is where most people and churches stop. They think this is the end goal and the farthest anyone can go. They're wrong. There is more.

This is where Hagberg and Guelich's concept of The Wall becomes helpful for us. There are other ways of describing The Wall throughout church history that apply to the same experience. You might have heard of "the dark night of the soul" as coined by Saint John of the Cross. Or it might be the "long dark corridor," as described by Teresa of Avila. While none of these are necessarily a one-to-one analog for deconstruction, they are all phenomenal descriptions that help us understand the *experience* of deconstruction. One way of thinking about deconstruction is someone hitting The Wall without having the resources in their faith to withstand it.

It's worth quoting Hagberg and Guelich at length here to get a sense of what The Wall is.

> When this stage comes, many feel propelled into it by an event outside of themselves. It's usually a crisis that turns their world upside down.
>
> If we have been people of strong faith, our life, though not necessarily easy, has fit nicely into our faith framework. Then the event or crisis often takes on major proportions. It often strikes close to our core, for example, our children, spouse, work, or health. For the first time, our faith does not seem to work. We feel remote, immobilized, unsuccessful, hurt, ashamed, or reprehensible. Neither our faith nor God provides what we need to soothe us, heal us, answer our prayers, fulfill our wishes, change our circumstances, or solve our problems. Our formula of faith, whatever that may have been, does not work anymore, or so it appears. We are stumped, hurting, angry, betrayed, abandoned, unheard, or unloved. Many simply want to give up. Their life of

faith may even seem to have been a fraud at worst, or a mirage at best.

Some enter this stage of the journey through a crisis in their faith more than in their personal lives. This is particularly true for people raised in churches with a clearly defined belief system, one with a strong code of conduct that provided guidance and answers for life and life's questions. . . .

Suddenly, something in one's strict adherence is called into question. One of the foundation blocks crumbles. Perhaps someone considered to be a model of faith, a person of genuine piety, is exposed for being involved in an immoral or illegal activity. Perhaps another way of looking at the Scriptures or relating to God and life begins to catch one's attention. For example, specific doctrines about Scripture or the Church's infallibility come into question. Gnawing questions become more and more unmanageable, questions about what we believe and have believed about how we live and why we do what we do and do not do certain things. We are no longer able to ignore or repress them. They haunt us continually. So much so that we become aware of a larger gap in our lives of faith. We sense ourselves slipping more and more into a period of limbo.[3]

Does any of that sound familiar? This is the experience of hitting The Wall. While not everyone who hits The Wall goes on to deconstruct their faith, you can imagine what this experience would be like for someone who has been raised in cultural Christianity, attends a compromised church, and has a life full of cumulative anxieties. Even just one of these would set someone up for disaster when they hit The Wall. It takes a deep spiritual well to hit The Wall and not panic or feel frightened by it.

For many, this is the beginning of deconstruction. But most believers and churches don't know about or acknowledge this experience of faith. When the lights turn off, and the floor drops out from under you, and you experience God's *absence*, not his presence, what do you do then?

Did you catch the word repeated three times in Hagberg and Guelich's description? *Crisis.* It's typically catalyzed by a personal crisis or a crisis of faith. The experience of hitting The Wall, of deconstructing, isn't a fun intellectual exercise, or an excuse to go about sinning (though, of course, it can be catalyzed by both of those, since a life of willful sin can produce a crisis of conscience that demands a choice be made). A crisis brings deconstruction about and is *itself* a crisis. This experience of hitting The Wall is what we talk about when we talk about deconstruction.

THE GRIEF OF LOSS

If you've ever lost a loved one to either death or estrangement, then you have an idea of what this feels like. One of the first people to talk about deconstruction as it is talked about now in a public way was "Science Mike" McHargue, one of the original founders of the popular podcast *The Liturgists* and author of the book *Finding God in the Waves*. In his book, McHargue tells his story of growing up in the church and his eventual deconstruction. Here is how he tells the part of his story when the trapdoor finally opened beneath him.

> That morning, I said these words: "God, I don't know why I'm praying. You aren't even real."
>
> Two things happened immediately. First, the feeling I associated with the presence of God left me, like a morning mist burned away by the heat of the sun. Second, I felt as if a trapdoor opened beneath me and I fell through it. A series of dark insights entered my mind with terrifying speed. I realized that all the people I had loved and who had died before me were gone. Forever. I'd never see them again, because the only thing waiting

on the other side of death was infinite blackness and the an-
nihilation of self.

There was no heaven. There was no hell. Beyond this life,
there was ... nothing. Without God, life had no objective
purpose. All those tough days I had pushed through, believing
that I served a higher purpose—that purpose was nothing but
a comforting self-delusion. My life was meaningless. So were
the lives of my children and of every person who had ever lived
or ever would. It didn't matter what kind of husband or father
I was, because all my hard work would be erased when the sun
exploded in four or five billion years.

I felt a profound grief, an inky-black darkness, as I realized
there was neither mission nor redemption for humanity. The
universe was indifferent to us. We were all just an accident of
the self-organizing principles of physics, mere quirks of gravity,
electromagnetism, and chemistry. This was it. This was the end
of my search. "God, I don't know why I'm praying. You aren't
even real." In the time it took to say those 11 words, I'd become
an existential nihilist.

And my parents got divorced anyway.[4]

For McHargue, deconstruction wasn't just an intellectual exercise.
The primary emotion wasn't curiosity. It was grief, angst, and fear.
Everything he thought he could trust disintegrated in an instant. The
foundation on which he had built his life had crumbled. When I
think back on my own experience and survey other deconstruction
stories, this is the common denominator that I see.

When you've spent your whole life believing God is your Father,
losing God isn't just losing an idea; it's like losing a parent. Losing a
parent is crushing and disorienting. It's one of the most difficult
things anyone will experience. The very people whose words weighed
the most, who you looked up to in awe and reverence, who impacted
your entire existence for good or for ill, are no longer there. Our

parents are some of the most powerful relationships in our lives. God relates to us the way our parents relate to us. If you lose God, you lose the stability, love, comfort, protection, and presence that is even better than what the best earthly father brings to their family.

Another thing that is lost is God's family, the church. You might have grown up in church and considered your church your family. Your closest friends were at church. Your social support was the church. But now, you don't know who you can trust. You feel like an outcast, whether because of your own internal feelings or because others have made you feel that way through their actions. You lose trust in the very people you trusted everything with. The community you had for years you no longer have and can no longer rely on. You find yourself isolated and alone, maybe even ostracized. A pariah of God's people.

But it's not just God and his people; you even feel like you've lost yourself. When you've spent your whole life "finding your identity in Christ," losing God means losing your very identity. If you aren't a Christian, someone who goes to church, reads their Bible, prays, serves others, or plays in the worship band—if that's not you, who are you?

And really, it's bigger and more fundamental than even your sense of self. When you lose God, you've lost an entire framework to understand reality. What is right and wrong? What is good and evil? How do you make decisions? The entire moral, ethical, and narrative framework by which you've understood the world has been pulled out from under you.

Now, you have lost someone as meaningful as a parent, you don't have a community to belong to, you don't have a sense of self, and you don't have a framework for understanding reality. What do you have left?

This is why deconstruction is so scary. It's as if all the lights in the room were turned off at the same time in the middle of the night. It's at this moment you find yourself entering the grieving process, grieving everything you've lost.

THE HIDDENNESS OF GOD

The reality is this: it is a normal part of the life of faith to experience the absence of God. The psalmist writes in Psalm 22:2, "My God, I cry by day, but you do not answer, by night, yet I have no rest." We don't experience the hiddenness of God because he is displeased with us. In his absence, our faith is tested, not because God doesn't know the quality of it, but because it's only through putting our faith to the test that our faith can *grow*. It's through the appearance of losing our faith that our faith is exercised.

Like a muscle is ripped in order to grow stronger, crises tear our faith, not to destroy it, but so that it can grow back stronger. It wasn't until after four hundred years of silence, after the prophet Malachi penned his final words, that God himself burst onto the scene in the human flesh of Jesus Christ. As Richard Foster writes, "In the very act of hiddenness, God is slowly weaning us of fashioning him in our own image. . . . By refusing to be a puppet on our string or a genie in our bottle, God frees us from our false, idolatrous images."[5]

We cannot continue to view The Wall—and the deconstruction it so often leads to—as something that someone sets out to do as an intellectual quest or an aberration from a normal life of faith. This *is* part of the life of faith. Not everyone will hit The Wall, and not everyone who does will hit it in the same way. Some will hit it suddenly and be there for a long time. Some will see it coming a mile away and move through it relatively quickly. Others will move through it gradually, bit by bit, over the course of their lives. You don't have to hit The Wall to become a mature Christian. But the experience of hitting The Wall is a normal one. Are our churches equipped to walk with people through The Wall? Are *we* equipped to walk with someone through The Wall? Are we even equipped to go through it *ourselves*?

How we view the life of faith makes all the difference. We need to have a spiritual realism about what it means to walk with Jesus through the realities of life. Either we have categories and language for this experience, or we will be blindsided, caught unaware by the hard knocks of life that break our categories and obscure our sight of God. The dark nights of the soul—the clouds of unknowing—are nearly unbearable, but they are a crucible of transformation that, if we allow, will deliver us to a renewed faith greater than we could have ever imagined.

DECONSTRUCTING
THE CRISIS

IF DECONSTRUCTION IS FIRST AND FOREMOST a crisis of faith, then we need to reorient how we think about it. It's tempting to think about it as a linear process, like backsliding and growth, where someone slides down and out of their faith into deconstruction and then grows back up into a stronger faith. From the outside, that might be what it looks like. But that isn't what the experience of deconstruction feels like.

Deconstruction isn't experienced as a linear journey but shares the experience of every other grieving process. There are five stages of grief that are commonly regarded to be the normative experience for people who go through it. The five stages (as Elisabeth Kübler-Ross and David Kessler famously described them) are denial, anger, bargaining, depression, and acceptance.[1]

Even though they're listed as stages, the five stages of grief are more like being in a pinball machine than on a train track. Each stage is experienced randomly; you have no control over which stage you are in, and there is no set length that each stage takes. You might be in the denial stage for five years and the anger stage for five days or vice versa.[2] Even after you have reached the acceptance stage, where you have accepted the loss and moved on, any experience in the future could trigger a past stage and put you right back where you were before, even if it's years later. Some people might skip a stage or two entirely and experience only two or three of them.

All of these stages are triggered by one crisis. That means one crisis of faith can be expressed in five completely different ways. It might seem that because someone is expressing their faith differently, they're no longer in the crisis, but that would be to misunderstand how we process grief. Someone might be acting completely different from how they were a year ago because they are in a different stage of grief. While it's not on you as the person walking with them to constantly be diagnosing which stage they might be in, it is helpful to understand the ways that their crisis of faith might be expressed in each stage. In this way you can minister to them in a way that meets them where they are in the process.

DENIAL

The first stage of deconstruction is a tricky one. As you might be able to tell from the word *denial*, someone might be in this stage of deconstruction and not even know it. There might have been an incident to place doubts in their mind, but they haven't fully acknowledged them yet.

In fact, not only have they not acknowledged their doubts, but they might start fighting against them. This may be conscious, but more likely than not, it's more subconscious. The person may not be actively aware of their denial, which makes it difficult to know that they have begun the process of deconstruction.

To make it even more difficult to recognize, when someone is in denial of their deconstruction, this can look to others like the person's faith is growing stronger than ever. They may double down on their ministry activities, pray more, read their Bible more, and serve more. They might even start receiving comments from others about how much they're growing in their faith. The trouble is that what looks like growth is actually fear. When doubts start to rise in a person's heart and mind, and they feel the things that they have always held dear slipping away from them, they do whatever they can to hold on.

The denial stage can be isolating. People may feel ashamed or embarrassed to admit that they are struggling with their faith. They may fear being judged or rejected by their religious community, so they keep their doubts and questions to themselves. This can lead to feelings of loneliness and disconnection, which can further exacerbate the person's crisis.

When doubts, fears, and concerns don't have any place to go and continue to build because a person is unable to express them in a safe environment, they eventually bubble up and become too big to ignore. This is when deconstruction moves out of the denial stage. Eventually, these doubts must be dealt with.

Denial, like each stage in the process, may take a short amount of time or may take years. While denial might be hard to spot, it's still possible to engage with those who are in denial by creating a safe environment for people to express their doubts and fears. When people are in denial, there is an opportunity to significantly decrease the intensity of the crisis they are experiencing. In later chapters, we will talk more about what this looks like.

But for now, let's assume that someone doesn't have a safe environment to express their doubts and questions. What happens next?

ANGER

When you think about the deconstruction movement as it's expressed in online spaces, or maybe even in some relationships that you have, this is the stage that you probably recognize the most. In the anger stage, people may lash out at the institutions, leaders, and practices they feel have betrayed or failed them. They may express their rage and frustration through confrontations, writing, speaking, or activism, seeking to hold these entities accountable for their experiences.

From the outside, it looks destructive. Bridges are being burned, relationships are being strained or ended, and the person is reacting to everything about the environment they were previously in. There is a lot of pendulum swinging in the anger stage. Anything that resembles the environment that they feel anger toward feels repulsive.

It's tempting to judge this person, and there are certainly ways that strong emotions can cause harm in this stage, but if the person is reacting to abuse—whether that's spiritual abuse, sexual abuse, or some other form—then anger is certainly warranted. It's possible that this person was abused or witnessed someone else being abused, spoke out about it, and felt ignored or pushed aside in order for others to cover for the abuser. Anger, in that case, is a natural response to bring attention to the dire need to correct a grave injustice.

In other cases, they might feel anger toward leaders for delivering them a faith that didn't deal with the difficulties of life. Maybe their faith didn't hold up under suffering or critical questions raised by secular scholarship. While their anger might be an overreaction toward people who had otherwise good intentions, it's understandable that they would feel resentment for not having the resources needed to navigate life's hardships when they were told that Jesus was all they needed.

It's all too easy for the stage of anger to be damaging and destructive. People may become consumed by their anger and may direct it to others who have not necessarily done anything wrong. They may engage in destructive behaviors, such as cutting ties with their communities or engaging in heated debates and arguments online with friends, family, and strangers. This can lead to further isolation and disconnection from others and may prevent them from being able to resolve their feelings of anger. As Kübler-Ross and Kessler say, "Anger is a natural reaction to the unfairness of loss. Unfortunately, however, anger can isolate you from friends and family at the precise time you may need them the most."[3]

The anger stage is a necessary part of the deconstruction process, as it allows people to express and release their emotions. "Underneath anger is pain."[4] That's important for being able to process the feelings that one has when experiencing the failures of a faith community.

However, it is important for people to find healthy outlets for their anger. The best outlet for anger is a non-anxious person who can handle the anger without feeling threatened. We'll discuss the importance of a non-anxious presence in later chapters. But for now, the role you play as the person who is walking with them is critical in this stage.

How you handle their anger might be the difference between them feeling heard and being challenged to see a different perspective, or feeling like all Christians are the same: scared of being confronted and only interested in holding on to power. The cynicism that is present in the anger stage is palpable.

For many people, this might be the longest stage of their deconstruction. Anger is a satisfying emotion because it *feels* productive. If you were hurt in an environment that had real issues, burning it down feels like the right thing to do—not only to hold those who hurt you accountable but also to save others from experiencing the same hurt.

It might be good to help this person find a different church while being patient with them. Their trust in the church and church leaders has been broken. Staying connected with them while they heal and work to regain trust is important. It's crucial to be able to cut through the cynicism and anger as someone who isn't scared but is confident in their faith and in their relationship with the person who is deconstructing.

BARGAINING

In many ways, bargaining might look and feel a lot like denial. Except this time, it's in the middle of the process instead of at the beginning. You're actively aware that you have been deconstructing. That's not news to you. However, bargaining can be an attempt to relieve the pain and tension of deconstruction. It's an attempt to take an early off-ramp. To short-circuit the process. But it is also a waypoint, a transition point in the deconstruction process. To quote Kübler-Ross and Kessler again, "Bargaining can help our mind move from one state of loss to another. It can be a way station that gives our psyche the time it may need to adjust. Bargaining may fill the gaps that our strong emotions generally dominate, which often keep suffering at a distance. It allows us to believe that we can restore order to the chaos that has taken over."[5]

This is where people try to make deals with God, doubling down on religious activities once again to prove that their faith is true and to avoid the pain of deconstruction. In the stage of bargaining, people may try to prove their faith to themselves and to others by engaging in religious activities with increased intensity and frequency. They may pray more, read their Bible more, attend church again, and serve more, hoping to find evidence of God's presence and to confirm the truth of their beliefs.

This is tricky because these are all good activities. In fact, continuing to participate in spiritual disciplines, community, and rituals might be one of the best things someone can do when God seems distant. The problem isn't so much in the actions themselves as much as the heart behind the actions. Someone patiently persevering through a season of spiritual dryness will perform all the same actions as someone who is trying to prove to themselves, others, or God that they really have faith. One comes from a deep trust in God's faithfulness while the other comes from a place of deep anxiety about their own faithfulness. We don't want to discourage the actions, but we do want to examine the heart.

Bargaining can be a desperate effort to avoid the discomfort and uncertainty of deconstruction. They might not be as angry as they were in the anger stage because they feel the isolation that it created and want to integrate back into a community. But this isn't reconstruction yet. It's an attempt to relieve the pressure of deconstruction without the work of reconstruction.

Deconstruction requires an intense amount of self-reflection and theological and cultural reprocessing. Without that work, someone will stay in deconstruction. It's possible that someone's life may begin to look very religiously active again while being in the bargaining phase of deconstruction.

No matter how hard people try to prove their faith through their actions, the reality of their deconstruction will eventually come floating back to the surface. This can lead to feelings of disillusionment and disappointment as people realize that their religious activities do not provide the security and comfort they were seeking. It may provide some short-term relief, but it ultimately hinders people's ability to engage with their doubts and explore new possibilities. By moving beyond bargaining, people can begin to accept the reality of their deconstruction and explore new ways of understanding and experiencing God than the ways they previously understood. We'll explore this more in part two of this book.

So how do you engage with people in the bargaining stage? On the one hand, you want to encourage them in their efforts to reintegrate into the community. This provides a wonderful opportunity for you to have important conversations with them as they want to be part of the community and are open to the things of the faith again. They are still carrying the hurt and pain that brought them into deconstruction in the first place, so you'll always want to be mindful of that.

However, at this point, they might be open to talking about how the Christian faith actually has resources for them in their pain. Always be gracious and intentional in your conversations, but you might begin to ask how the resources they have for dealing with their pain are working. If they've left behind a bodily resurrection for a spiritual resurrection, how does that give them hope in times of darkness? Can it really hold the weight? How do they feel attending a church that holds to beliefs they say they no longer hold themselves? Do they feel any tension with that? How do they reconcile that?

The bargaining stage is a time when someone might be open to doubting their doubts. It's only possible for someone to doubt one belief if they are weighing it against another belief that they aren't doubting.[6] Many doubts are born out of an implicit acceptance of another belief that hasn't been recognized yet. In many cases, someone

hasn't deconstructed enough because they haven't doubted these under-
lying implicit beliefs that have created the doubts they're wrestling
with. Without trying to control them, a series of good questions might
be able to create doubts about their doubts that alter their journey.

When I was in my bargaining phase of deconstruction, I was involved in a parachurch ministry but not a church. I'll never forget the
time when a man who was a few years older than me and who I respected texted me out of nowhere. He told me, as silly as it sounds today,
that he unfollowed me on Instagram. At the time, that felt like a big
deal. When I asked him why, he said that it was because I always talked
about what the church should and shouldn't be doing and posted about
all the ministries I was involved in, but I wasn't involved in a church
myself. He said he couldn't take someone seriously who talked a big
game about the church but wasn't involved in one personally.

I had no skin in the game. It was tough love, but he was right, and
I knew it. It's what I needed to hear. After that, I began looking for a
church and attending one, becoming heavily involved. That ended up
becoming its own story of church hurt over the course of the next five
years. But the point here is that it changed my perspective and the
course of my deconstruction. I was no longer doing it outside the
church but inside the church. Did my faith immediately become
stronger after that? No. But it put me on a course I wasn't on before
that would take me, after a long time, to where I needed to be.

Years later, I was texting this man and told him that—through that
text—he changed my life. Having my own hypocrisy pointed out to me
in love by someone I knew, respected, and trusted—while I was busy
pointing out the hypocrisy of the church—helped me see that if I was
serious about resolving my own doubts, critiques, and pain, then I
would need to do it in community, in the church, not alone on my own.

My bargaining phase was the least turbulent of my deconstruction.
It even looked the most religious. But it was also the most crucial.
Without seeing how all the ways I was trying to hide and help were

actually exposing me and hurting others even more, I wouldn't have been put on the course of my eventual reconstruction.

DEPRESSION

In the depression stage, people may experience a deep sense of loss, isolation, and even resignation as they come to terms with the fact that their beliefs no longer feel reliable or meaningful. This stage is full of terrible "aha" moments. In fact, this stage might often come directly after denial because, after they can no longer deny their doubts and what is happening to their faith, the harsh reality sets in.

"Maybe God isn't real after all."

"Maybe the Bible isn't reliable."

"Maybe I can't trust anyone in my church."

"Maybe this thing has always been a sham."

A terrible feeling of having been duped for their whole life sets in. Depending on their involvement in the church, they might even feel guilt and shame for thinking they duped others.

It's different from anger. In anger, intense emotions move outward toward others. In depression, the emotions move inward toward the self. They'll start to feel disconnected from their communities and God. This can be a painful and isolating experience, as people may feel like they have lost a fundamental part of their identity and sense of purpose. They may question their own worth and value. If they're not loved by God, how can they be loved at all? This can feel devastating, as people may feel like there is no way out of their pain and suffering.

They may feel like they are trapped in a cycle of depression and that God has abandoned them. Shame, for many people, is an overwhelming feeling in their deconstruction. The shame might come from even having those doubts in the first place. It might come from feeling ostracized by the community. It might come from feeling like something is wrong with them that they can't just simply *believe* like everyone else seems to believe. Through isolation and shame, it's normal for people to become stuck; to resign to the feeling that there is no way out of this, that there's no point in trying to resolve the pain they feel in losing God and their community.

In some cases, not all, but in some, depression may even manifest itself in paranoia. If someone has experienced abuse in the church, there might be good reasons for them to feel paranoid. But for others, their paranoia about all things related to faith and the church might be an attempt to preserve their sense of safety by avoiding something that has caused pain in the past.

So, how do you engage with someone in the depression stage of deconstruction? Continue to engage with them. You might have to be the one to initiate as they will want to withdraw from the process. Don't be pushy with your engagement but walk with them as a friend. Help them see their questions and doubts as things that are outside of them and don't reflect on their value, dignity, and worth.

Deconstruction is a process that needs to be leaned into, not away from. You can only move beyond your doubts and pain by moving through them. Help them continue the journey and to see value in not resigning to an unfinished process but to push forward.

The depression stage is a natural part of the deconstruction process. How could you not feel a sense of depression when everything you've known and loved now feels false and maybe even harmful? But this is an opportunity to help people know that they are still loved and there is still value in the pursuit of truth, and that if they press on, the reward will be greater than if they stay where they are.

ACCEPTANCE

Finally, there is the acceptance phase. In this phase, we release our attachment to our old beliefs and accept the outcome of our deconstruction, whatever that may be. This may involve replacing our faith, remixing it, or renewing it.

We'll be going into the acceptance stage more in-depth in a future chapter. The important thing to keep in mind, for now, is that while in the process of deconstruction, in the mind of the person who is deconstructing, there is no predetermined outcome. You can't enter deconstruction expecting to have a stronger faith on the other side. The only way through deconstruction is a commitment to follow the truth through the darkness. But there are ways to create fertile soil for a renewed faith that we will discuss later.

The experience of deconstruction is not a linear and predictable journey. This can make the process of deconstruction unpredictable and confusing and can make it difficult for people to know what to expect. By understanding what they are going through, you know how to best interact with them in each stage and be a faithful, loving, presence in their lives.

It's in the context of a crisis of faith that we find deconstruction. Not as a cold examination of beliefs, but as the loss of hope and the desperate need to make sense of the grief we are experiencing.

DECONSTRUCTING BELIEF

WHEN YOU HEAR THE WORD "DECONSTRUCTION," the first word you probably associate with it is "doubt." As we've established, deconstruction is more than doubt. It's the existential, spiritual crisis that comes with doubt. But while it's *more* than doubt, it certainly isn't *less* than doubt. Becoming aware of your doubts—and more importantly, being frightened by your doubts—is usually the first tip-off that you might be deconstructing your faith.

One of the first things you will find in deconstruction circles is the valorization of doubt. To doubt means that you are finally thinking for yourself, taking your faith into your own hands, and leaving behind the shackles of fundamentalism. Like former Christian artist Michael Gungor said in his book, *The Crowd, the Critic and the Muse*, "Doubt purifies faith. Without doubt, belief calcifies into rigid fundamentalism. Without doubt, there are no questions; and without questions, there is no imagination."[1] For Gungor and many others, without doubt, your faith might be toxic, but with doubt, your faith will be purified. But is doubt really a virtue? Does a lack of doubt stifle an imaginative faith?

After Jesus had risen from the dead, he showed himself to his disciples. They saw his risen body and he breathed the Holy Spirit onto them. But one disciple was missing: Thomas. Thomas infamously doubted Jesus' resurrection until he could see Jesus for himself. He told his fellow disciples, "If I don't see the mark of the nails in his hands, put my finger into the mark of the nails, and put my hand into his side, I will never believe" (John 20:25). Without seeing, he would never believe.

A week later, Jesus appeared to the disciples again. This time, Thomas was there. Graciously, Jesus prompted Thomas to see the marks from the nails in his hands and to touch his side where the spear had pierced him. Upon seeing the evidence, Thomas proclaimed, "My Lord and my God!" And Jesus responded to him, "Because you have seen me, you have believed. Blessed are those who have not seen and yet believe" (John 20:26-29).

Jesus' response to doubt was twofold: first, he obliged the doubtful request and showed the evidence. He didn't hide himself from Thomas or denounce him as a disciple for doubting. However, he didn't valorize his doubt either. He didn't commend Thomas as being virtuous for demanding the evidence. Thomas wasn't shamed for doubting, but Jesus blessed those who didn't doubt.

The Israelites in the Old Testament foreshadowed this. Almost immediately after Israel had made a covenant with the Lord at Mount Sinai, which was right after he powerfully and miraculously liberated them from captivity in Egypt, they doubted whether YHWH—who they did not see—was truly the almighty God, and whether Moses was truly his faithful messenger. "Come, make gods for us who will go before us because this Moses, the man who brought us up from the land of Egypt—we don't know what has happened to him!" (Exodus 32:1). In their doubt and impatience, Israel forsook the God who had just rescued them from slavery and who had chosen them to be his own people, and they fashioned a god made in their own image that they could see with their eyes and touch with their hands.

Both Thomas and Israel, in their doubt, missed God. God graciously preserved his relationship with them through their doubt, maintained his covenant with them, and revealed himself to them. But in neither case was their doubt something to be celebrated. Jesus had told the disciples time and time again of his coming death and resurrection. Why didn't Thomas trust Jesus? God had just liberated Israel from four hundred years of slavery by the Egyptians and chosen them as his "treasured possession"; why did they doubt him so quickly? As it turns out, it might have been easier to get Israel out of Egypt than it would be to get the "Egypt" out of Israel.

IMAGINATIVE GRIDLOCK

What was it about "Egypt" that was stuck in the Israelites' psyche that, even while they saw God move mightily before their very eyes, they would so easily doubt his presence and goodness, leading them to turn from him to their own idols? In the book *A Failure of Nerve*, the late family therapist Edwin Friedman applies his wealth of insight into family systems theory to everything from individual relationships to entire nations and societies. In it, he coins the phrase "a nonanxious presence." Friedman posits that in order to have healthy, functioning relationships, organizations, communities, institutions, and societies, we need well-differentiated leaders who act as a nonanxious presence in the face of chronic emotional anxiety.

When he talks about anxiety, he isn't referring to clinical anxiety. He's talking about an emotional climate. People can be chronically anxious in their own lives when they aren't able to differentiate their emotions from the needs of others and worries of life. Another word for it would be *reactivity*. Someone is chronically anxious when they are highly reactive to external stimuli. Groups of chronically anxious people can come together and can unwittingly create anxious environments.

When someone is stuck in a chronically anxious environment, they can become what Friedman calls "imaginatively gridlocked." In fact, an entire community can suffer from imaginative gridlock. All they see is what is in front of them, and they can't imagine anything else. When this happens, the individuals within the community and the community itself become emotionally stuck, codependent on one another in unhealthy ways, and seemingly unable to escape.

How do you know when a person or community has a gridlocked imagination? Friedman puts forward three interlocking characteristics:

1. An unending treadmill of trying harder
2. Looking for answers instead of reframing questions
3. Either-or thinking that creates false dichotomies[2]

Think about the conditions Israel lived under while they were slaves in Egypt. Exodus tells us that while they were slaves (which was already a horrible condition to be in), they asked to go to the desert to worship the Lord for three days, and Pharaoh said to them, "You are slackers. Slackers! That is why you are saying, 'Let us go sacrifice to the LORD.' Now get to work. No straw will be given to you, but you must produce the same quantity of bricks" (Exodus 5:17-18). They could never do enough to satisfy the demands of Pharaoh. Israel was on an unending treadmill of trying harder.

When Israel was finally on the edge of the Red Sea, moments from their final escape, and saw the Egyptians pursuing them, they cried out to Moses, "Is it because there are no graves in Egypt that you have taken us away to die in the wilderness? What have you done to us by bringing us out of Egypt?" (Exodus 14:11). In their panic and the anxiety of the moment, they wanted answers. Uncomfortable in the space between slavery and freedom, instead of saying, "I saw God rescue us from Egypt with the plagues, I wonder how he will rescue us from the Egyptian army?" they wanted Moses to answer for what they perceived he had done to them—bringing them out of Egypt only to die.

From their perspective, there were only two options. "Isn't this what we told you in Egypt: Leave us alone so that we may serve the Egyptians? It would have been better for us to serve the Egyptians than to die in the wilderness" (Exodus 14:12). Even though they had already seen God's mighty hand, they couldn't fathom life on the other side of the Red Sea. They had no imagination of what it meant to be free. They had a false dichotomy: be slaves or die.

Israel was an imaginatively gridlocked community because of the
environment they had existed in for generations. For four hundred
years, they had no identity except as *slaves*. Now, they were being
freed, but couldn't comprehend what a life of freedom looked like.
They were stuck in their old identity with no vision of a future that
could be different. Unable to differentiate their old identity from their
new situation, they fell right back into what was natural for them:
gods they could see and touch, just like the gods of Egypt.

Many Christians and churches have become imaginatively gridlocked. They've lost a vision of what it means to live a Christian life.
But how? What has captured their imagination in such a way that
they've lost sight of Christ and his call on our lives?

MORALISTIC THERAPEUTIC DEISM

Christian Smith famously coined the phrase *moralistic therapeutic
deism* in 2005 as the default set of beliefs of most Americans. Smith
posited five statements that make up moralistic therapeutic deism.

1. A God exists who created and ordered the world and watches
   over human life on earth.

2. God wants people to be good, nice, and fair to each other, as
   taught in the Bible and by most world religions.

3. The central goal of life is to be happy and to feel good about
   oneself.

4. God does not need to be particularly involved in one's life
   except when God is needed to resolve a problem.

5. Good people go to heaven when they die.[3]

Many people who are deconstructing were raised in churches or
homes that, perhaps unwittingly, promoted these views. These beliefs
stand in stark contrast to the Christian gospel.

The first belief is, of course, correct and foundational to Christian
belief. After that, things start to fall apart. God does desire us to be
good and righteous, but our goodness on its own is not enough. We

are dead in our trespasses and sins. We aren't just bad people that need to be good, we're dead people that need to be made alive by God's Spirit. That is *not* something taught by other world religions and secular philosophies.

The Bible never teaches that the goal of life is to be happy and feel good about oneself. In fact, Jesus makes it clear that Christians are to take up their crosses and follow him, that we will have trouble in this world, and that life might not always be up and to the right for us. God *is* involved in our lives even when we aren't aware of it. He isn't simply a divine problem solver when we need him; he is our Lord and King, to whom we submit every inch of our lives. And when we die, only those who are in Christ will be with God, not anyone who did "enough" good things. But even then, this completely ignores that heaven is not our final destination. We will live forever in the new creation, in resurrected bodies, with Christ as our King. There will be nothing ethereal about our final state. We will be embodied just as we are today but with new, imperishable, and glorious bodies.

Moralistic therapeutic deism is the hyperindividualization of religion and is the bread and butter of cultural Christianity. It turns the truths of Christianity around and holds them under the light of the self. "How does this serve me?" is the subliminal question asked by those caught in its grip. It substitutes reality and faithfulness for self-actualization and pragmatism. The beliefs of moralistic therapeutic deism have infiltrated the church at such a scale that questioning them almost seems like heresy in and of itself. Yet when they make up the foundation of our faith more than the truths revealed in Scripture, it's no wonder that our house of faith isn't sturdy.

Different names for the same thing. Moralistic therapeutic deism (MTD) has shown up in a few different flavors—most obviously in the pop evangelicalism of the early 2000s. The seeker-sensitive movement that traded Scripture for tips and tricks, discipleship for growth, and character for power is the prime example of trading the gospel for MTD, growing their churches by helping people live better, happier lives instead of taking up their crosses and following Jesus.

But there are other ways that MTD has been adopted, in less obvious ways. For example, conservatives have adopted a sort of MTD in how they teach about the law, grace, and society. They insist on a narrow set of morals in order to please God. If you live within this set of morals, then God will bless you, and you will have a good life. If you sin, God will curse you, and you will suffer. The central goal of life is said to be obeying God, but the result of obeying God is thought to be a happy, good life. So, the goal isn't truly obedience but happiness, just like in MTD.

The flip side of conservative MTD is progressive MTD. Progressives replace the pietistic, personal morality of the conservatives with social ethics. What makes you a good person isn't how you conduct your personal life, but your activism in dismantling oppressive and unjust systems. Progressives tend to be less concerned about obeying God in order to please him and are more interested in finding their "true self" and expressing it. They believe that life is about minimizing suffering and being happy. So, for progressives, the therapeutic part is literal. Therapy has become the pathway to shedding all of the false stories, trauma, and roadblocks that keep us from discovering our true selves. God's role in both justice and healing from trauma is incidental at best. If there isn't tangible evidence of justice and healing through reformed systems and therapy, then God isn't given much thought.

Both of these expressions of moralistic therapeutic deism gridlock someone's imagination into narrow, specific ideas of what it means to be a Christian. Both are never-ending treadmills of trying harder. Both demand some form of certainty, whether it's doctrinal, moral, or ethical. Both pit the private expression of faith and the public implications of faith against each other.

The truth is that God cares about both the conservative and the progressive concerns. He cares about our bedrooms and our wallets, our personal holiness and our public systems, our piety and our justice.

But the danger of moralistic therapeutic deism isn't simply emphasizing the wrong things. When either of these expressions of MTD are left to ferment in someone's faith, one of two things can happen: the faith becomes so watered down that it stops mattering entirely, or in an attempt to protect their sense of happiness and moral superiority, it solidifies around itself and becomes fundamentalist.

In both scenarios, the person's imagination of the Christian life has been gridlocked by lies about what it really is. It doesn't matter if the person is conservative or progressive; both have been captured by a system that makes them more anxious by demanding works, withholding grace, seeking certainty, and forcing false dichotomies.

Someone might recognize the irrelevance of such a system and quietly drop it, or they might become so anxious by it that they seek a way to break free. The human spirit wasn't meant to be confined in such tight, graceless systems. Many people are starting to see it for what it is: an endless treadmill of trying harder.

A STIFLED FAITH

If someone's faith has been imaginatively gridlocked by the environment they have been in through some form of moralistic therapeutic deism, then it makes sense that at some point cracks will begin to form and the system will begin to break. Think about your church, a past church, your friend, child, or congregant. Have there been dominant cultural or relational dynamics that have lacked grace and space to breathe, relax, and simply *be*? It might not even be the whole church, but the specific segment of the church that this person spent most of their time in. Would it be aptly described as an unending treadmill of trying harder?

It might have been because of a perpetual fear of sin or hell. Maybe it was a need to be or appear perfect, so that people felt like they couldn't be the flawed, fallible humans they are. Has anyone in your life described their church experience with words like "burnout," "I couldn't breathe," "repressed," or "perfectionist"? Do they feel like no matter what they did, it would never be good enough for God, their pastors, their friends, or maybe even you? Do they feel like they must hide their flaws and imperfections, put on a face, and keep trying to make God and everyone else happy?

What about the ability to ask questions? Is there a constant need for certainty or at least to project certainty? Are doubts and questions welcomed to be explored, or are they looked down on and stuffed? Are things that don't matter much asserted with such force that it feels like life or death to ask questions? Are answers framed in terms of modern cultural assumptions and a simplistic "plain reading of the text," or are they reframed to be in light of the questions the Bible is seeking to answer (which might not be the ones we want to be answered in our culture)?

What about the way certain doctrines or ethical beliefs are presented? Are they presented as a binary either-or choice that creates false dichotomies? Is there any space for living in tension, searching for nuance, and reckoning with the maddening complexities of life that look more gray than black and white? Or are there attitudes of "if you're not with me, then you're my enemy"?

If you read those descriptions and think, "That actually *does* describe the church or relationship this person is experiencing," then you might be looking at a church or relationship that is imaginatively gridlocked, and, therefore, so is the person who deconstructed. Only one way of being a Christian has been presented to them. The person, in their grief, isn't able to reconcile what they are experiencing internally with the gridlock they exist in. They feel they only have two options: stay in the very thing that is suffocating them or break away entirely, leaving the whole thing behind just to breathe.

THE UNRAVELING SWEATER

It's in this context of a gridlocked imagination and the sandy foundation of moralistic therapeutic deism that faith can easily unravel like a sweater. When doctrines are mere accessories to a faith that is ultimately centered around the individual, and something from outside of that system smashes through and contradicts or undermines a held belief and seems to provide a better path to a happy, moral life than the belief they hold, everything comes apart. Anything not deemed necessary—or contrary to—moralistic therapeutic deism is cast aside.

The first and most obvious example of this is hell. Hell, for many who are deconstructing, is often one of the first doctrines to be questioned. How can a good God who created humans that he loves, knowing that they would be born into a world of sin, condemn someone to an eternity of punishment if they don't put their trust in him? This reality is incredibly uncomfortable if the only framework you have is moralistic therapeutic deism. There's nothing happy about it, and it can even seem immoral from our vantage point.

Something similar could be said for a doctrine like penal substitutionary atonement. It's common for deconstruction circles to deem this doctrine "cosmic child abuse" because of the way it's often taught. The idea that God the Father would kill his Son on our behalf doesn't exactly sound like amazing grace—it sounds like abuse. This might be particularly hard for someone who comes from a family where the father was abusive or was absent entirely. It sounds all too familiar for all the wrong reasons.

Anxious environments only allow for narrow interpretations of Scripture that force people into false either-or dichotomies. This is seen most clearly in how one interprets Genesis 1. In many cases, the only interpretation that is offered is a literal, six-day, young-earth creation. People are told that if Genesis 1 isn't a literal account of how God made the world, then none of the rest of the Bible is trustworthy.

The same is true for the book of Revelation. Many were raised with an interpretation of Revelation that had them looking to current events for signs of the coming antichrist, awaiting a rapture that would sweep them out of this world just in time to miss the great tribulation before Jesus returns. That is, of course, one way of interpreting the strange book that is Revelation. But it is not the only faithful way to do so. Yet some environments make that interpretation core to their beliefs and don't allow for any deviation. For them, questioning the rapture is tantamount to denying Christ himself.

Once you've started unraveling doctrines like hell, creation, the atonement, end times, and the trustworthiness of Scripture, the sweater continues to unravel. The stories of the Old Testament fall into question, the significance of Paul's writings is diminished, the goodness of the historic Christian sexual ethic is put on trial, and finally, the physical resurrection of Jesus himself is either spiritualized to be meaningless or done away with entirely. The sweater has unraveled and is no longer wearable. There's nothing left to do except to cast it aside.

Of course, this journey looks different for different people. Any one of those doctrines could go in any order, but the path is usually remarkably similar. When you're in a gridlocked environment, you have no sense of the outside world. Faithful Christians who think differently than the system you're in seem unimaginable. Exploring other traditions doesn't seem like an option. The only way out is to *break* out. To deconstruct it down to the bare bones and examine each part on its own. The anxiety created by the gridlock is too much to hold. Everything falls apart.

5

DECONSTRUCTING CHURCH

Every institution is in crisis, not just the church. Trust in institutions is at a generational low across the board. Whether it's the church, the government, schools, the family, or almost any other institution, they simply aren't seen as important or good for society's flourishing as they once were. It might seem strange to start a chapter about the church by talking about institutions more generally, but the truth is that institutions mediate our life experiences, so it's a dangerous place to be when people's trust in institutions is through the floor.

Institutions exist to preserve ideas, ideals, relationships, missions, and visions that are beyond any single individual. We might bristle at the idea of institutions as a dusty relic to be left on a shelf, but our entire lives are lived in relationship to institutions. This means that far from abandoning institutions (which is impossible), we should be more interested in the health of our institutions.

In his book *A Time to Build*, political analyst Yuval Levin wrote about how our institutions have eroded over the course of a century. He argues that because institutions give our common life shape by structuring it through values, habits, and interactions, institutions are inherently *formative* in nature. And indeed, that's their purpose: not simply to mediate our lives but to shape our character. Institutions function like molds that we pour ourselves into, take on their shape, and solidify our character in their image. When I became a father, fatherhood required certain things of me in order to care and provide for my son. The role of father formed me into a certain kind of person just by virtue of the demands it placed on my life. Institutions function in the same way. Institutions exist to form us.

However, we've started seeing our institutions differently, and so our institutions are taking on a different role in our lives. Instead of seeing institutions as molds to form us, we have begun seeing institutions as platforms to perform on. Going back to the parenthood analogy, you see this on social media with people using their children as content to build platforms as parenting influencers. Instead of allowing parenthood to form them into certain kinds of people, they are using their children to perform for others. The same thing has happened to our institutions. Instead of being *formative*, institutions have become *performative*. Instead of allowing ourselves to be shaped by them, we take advantage of them to gain the attention of others and build our own notoriety. Instead of existing to preserve ideals that are bigger than any individual, we co-opt the institution to platform our own ideals. It becomes a stage for our expressive individualism and quest for self-actualization. When this happens, the institution loses its trust and credibility as it fades into the shadow of the individuals who care nothing about it except as a stage to dance on.

We need our institutions to be strong, formative influences. Institutions hold us together, absorb our anxieties, and give structure to our lives. There is a direct correlation between the strength of our institutions and the stability of our lives. Without healthy institutions, we experience personal crises. Levin writes, "A crisis of institutions would present itself perhaps most powerfully as a crisis of our inner lives—of despair and isolation, loneliness, and loss of purpose. Such social shapelessness is how we can be at once too confrontational and too lonely, in touch with everyone and yet untouched by anyone, alienated together. It is how everyone can claim the mantle of the outsider at the same time. It results from the lack of place, connection, and belonging that are functions not just of being alone but also of being adrift, denied roles that might help us fit as parts into a larger whole."[1] Sound familiar?

Individuals who use institutions to perform—rather than be formed by them—are the rain and the wind that erode the soil of institutions. As they become weaker and weaker, their formative resources are stripped from them, leaving them a shell of their potential and a shadow of their purpose. We are losing the molds that shape our character and bring us together.

With that in mind, it's not a big leap to see how compromised churches become performative institutions. Many churches have become platforms for identity performance in at least three specific ways: (1) attractionalism, (2) the covering up of abuse, and (3) the embrace of partisan politics. These distortions of the church erode its formative power and leave its congregants as unformed, untethered individuals.

Mark Zuckerberg, founder and CEO of Meta, famously made the unofficial slogan for Facebook "Move fast and break things." While no church would outright say that, there has been a tacit acceptance of this mentality in much of American evangelicalism. In the name of reaching the lost, there has been a willingness to throw people under the bus who would rather move slower and focus on discipleship than "do anything short of sin" to reach as many people as possible.

The things that are broken aren't just products, systems, or norms, but people. If someone's outcry of abuse gets in the way of the "mission" or might threaten someone's reputation, well, move fast and break things. If someone needs years to work through doubt and uncertainty, move fast and break things. Anything that stands in the way of the performers performing is a barrier to be broken. This move-fast-and-break-things mentality leads you down the road to a diluted cultural Christianity.

ATTRACTIONALISM

At the heart of attractional churches is an attempt to bottle up a spiritual experience and reproduce it week after week for the purpose of making Christianity more appealing and for attracting more people to their church.[2] What do I mean by "attractional"? I like how pastor and author Jared Wilson describes it: "An attractional church conducts worship and ministry according to the desires and values of potential consumers. This typically leads to the dominant ethos of pragmatism throughout the church."[3] The emphasis leans heavily on this experiential aspect, operating under the assumption that the emotional resonance of the experience can create change in people's lives.

It's worth noting that attractionalism has little to do with the size of a church. Churches of all sizes, big and small, can succumb to the pragmatic poison of attractionalism. Likewise, churches of all sizes can resist the temptation to be performative. This isn't about a church's size as much as it's about a church's culture.

The problem is that this approach abandons the formative aspects of the institution for the experiential. Shifting from formative to performative has caused the Sunday service and the experience it provides to take precedence over the formative and liturgical structure of the service and the church as a whole, attracting people to an experience rather than molding them into the character of Christ. The result of this shift has been substantial church growth in terms of attendance numbers because of the low bar for entry, minimal demands on congregants, and personality-driven culture, but a shallow and individualistic faith for those who attend the church. This, of course, has downstream effects.

Biblical illiteracy. When a performative church creates consumers instead of disciples, there isn't much of a perceived need for the Bible in their life. They might read a daily devotional with a verse or two plucked out of context, or hear the passage read for the sermon on Sunday, but there is little or no deep engagement with the Bible. In fact, in the study on dechurching, only 22 percent of cultural Christians said that "the Bible is the literal word of God" and, almost unbelievably, only 1 percent said that "Jesus is the Son of God."[4]

Scripture has the highest authority in the life of the Christian as it is God's very words to us. But performative churches opt more for programs around felt needs rather than the ministry of the Word. They don't "equip the saints for the work of ministry, to build up the body of Christ, until we all reach unity in the faith and in the knowledge of God's Son, growing into maturity with a stature measured by Christ's fullness" (Ephesians 4:12-13). The saints aren't equipped, the body of Christ isn't built up, there is no unity in the faith and knowledge of God's Son, and people are not growing into maturity measured by Christ.

The result is that the Christians in these churches simply don't know their Bibles. They are like "little children, tossed by the waves and blown around by every wind of teaching, by human cunning with cleverness in the techniques of deceit" (Ephesians 4:14). With no foundation to stand on, they give themselves over to the whims of their leaders, hoping they are leading them into truth. But because they don't know and can't be sure, if their leader *were* to ever betray that trust, the people would be incentivized to either cover up their leader's sin, because it would be pragmatically harmful for the church to acknowledge such sin, or to leave the faith completely because their faith was in the leader or the church, not in Christ himself.

Legalism and licentiousness. Another way attractionalism erodes discipleship is by leading people toward either legalism or licentiousness. Because pragmatism, not faithfulness, has become the center of the church, legalism and licentiousness become two sides of a spectrum that exert their gravitational pull on the spiritually anemic congregant. Instead of being rooted in the gospel and sustained by the Word of God, people suspect one of two things: either that the Christian life is all about being a good person, or that since they are "saved" they can do whatever they want.

Those who end up on the legalist side of things run themselves into the ground trying to be a good person but never understanding the gospel of grace in their lives. In turn, this also makes them more judgmental, as they try to hold everyone else to the same standards they themselves try to uphold. Everything is black and white, and there is no patience for understanding the complexities and hardships of people's lives.

This is the group that things like purity culture spring up from. In purity culture, you have a sort of sexual prosperity gospel, teaching that you will have a wonderful marriage, incredible children, and a satisfying sex life if only you will save yourself for marriage. Rather than hold up God's design for sexuality and all its beauty, purity culture makes empty promises it can't fulfill and shames those who fall short of its standard.

Purity culture has had damaging consequences on both men and women, but much more so on women who, as young girls, were given illustrations comparing them to chewed-up gum, destroyed roses, and tape that has lost its stick. Men were told that their sexual drive was far too strong and untamable—almost animalistic. Their only hope was to shape up, get accountability, and find a wife as soon as they could to channel their sexual energy into holy matrimony.

These dynamics led to shame for both sexes as they were essentially set up for failure. Either they went too far with their boyfriend or girlfriend and were constantly worried that they'd never get married because they were now worthless, or they actually made it to the "finish line" of marriage only to discover that all of what they were promised—marriage, children, sex—were more difficult than they imagined, leaving them to wonder if they did something wrong along the way, or if there was something wrong with *them*. Far from valuing women and men as God's image bearers, purity culture perpetuated the very objectification it was trying to thwart.

Those who are more on the licentious side reveal how little they believe the whole thing to begin with by disregarding Christ's call on their lives. This is rampant in cultural Christianity. To quote the study on dechurching again, cultural Christians "score comparatively low on their concern for ethical matters like discrimination, abortion, pornography, substance abuse, lying, stealing, and greed. However, they have an elevated prosperity gospel score, revealing that they might associate moral behaviors with material rewards of health and wealth. This dissonance hints at their lack of key gospel concepts."[5]

This leaves them as the arbiter of personal morality, only opting for private morals that suit them and their desires. The Christian call to holiness is relativized, making morality a free-for-all. It shouldn't be surprising that children raised in these homes see their parents disregarding the moral teachings of Scripture and conclude that, if their parents don't actually believe it despite calling themselves Christian and occasionally attending church, it must not be all that important, much less *real*. Who can blame them for giving up on something their parents never took seriously in the first place?

Many churches that should be formative institutions for congregants have become platforms for the personalities of pastors, worship leaders, and influential figures. Instead of embodying ideals, they express personalities. This leaves the church neglecting its primary duty: to form its congregants into the character of Christ.

ABUSE AND COVER-UPS

When talking about why people are leaving the church and the faith in droves, you can't ignore the issue of abuse and cover-ups within religious institutions. This is often one of the most cited reasons for someone who is deconstructing or leaving the faith.

In *The Great Dechurching*, the study showed that

> exvangelicals in our survey scored 74 percent higher on having experienced a lack of love from their congregations than the other four groups combined. On top of that, they scored twice as high as any other group on "negative experiences you

personally had in an evangelical church." To imagine the frustration and righteous anger of knowing that your daughter has been sexually assaulted and nothing will ever be done about it is to start to understand the perspective of some exvangelicals. If this or other religious abuses or abandonment happened to your family, wouldn't you become a church casualty too?[6]

It's impossible to guarantee total protection from all abuse, rampant abuse, and abuse being covered up, and it can easily happen in an institution that has been compromised by performative leaders. Leaders and institutions that cover up for abusers and fail to help the abused are putting their own perception above the injustice that has been perpetrated against an innocent image bearer of God. The church, in its ideal formative state, aims to shape its congregants into the character of Christ. This formation process leaves no room for abuse, let alone the concealment of abuse. For Christians, all sin, iniquity, and abuse should be brought into the light. Abuse or exploitation of others, and protecting those who perpetrate such acts, is fundamentally inconsistent with Christ's teachings. The church should be a sanctuary for the most vulnerable, offering them care, protection, and even honor.

However, this frequently has not been the case. Where should we start? The Catholic Church, the Southern Baptist Convention, Kanakuk Kamps, Bill Hybels, Ravi Zacharias, Hillsong, Mark Driscoll, James MacDonald, Jerry Falwell Jr., Mike Pilavachi? There are more names I could add since I wrote the first draft of this chapter. We could go on and on, and these examples are only recent ones that were highly publicized. They don't even scratch the surface of the abuse that flies under the public radar because it happens in smaller churches with pastors and leaders you have never heard of all across the United States. You've never read an article on the abuse I've personally witnessed in the church. But it doesn't make it any less real.

There are two things that pastors and leaders tend not to realize:

1. They inherently hold power in every relationship simply due to the fact of their position.[7]

2. When people experience abuse at the hands of someone else in the church, that abuse does not simply reflect the abuser or even the church; it reflects on God himself.

Christian psychologist Diane Langberg writes, "Abusive power has a profound impact on our relationship with God and with others. Victims of abuse often view God through a gravely distorted lens, seeing him as the source of the evil they experience. The violation and destruction of faith at times of tremendous suffering is one of the greatest tragedies of the abuse of power."[8]

Abuse destroys lives, and it destroys faith. When the shepherds who are tasked with the care of the sheep exploit and abuse them instead, they are the very wolves who devour the sheep that Scripture warns us about. When the church enables and protects abusers, it becomes an outpost of hell rather than the outpost of heaven it was intended to be. If someone can't trust those who represent God, how can they be expected to trust God himself?

EMBRACING PARTISAN POLITICS

On June 1, 2019, the choir at First Baptist Church of Dallas debuted a new song at the beginning of their Sunday service titled "Make America Great Again." In a stunning move, one of the largest churches in the United States not only endorsed the most controversial presidential candidate in modern history but wrote a song using his slogan to open a Sunday worship service. Obviously, this example is extreme, but few things typify the church's embrace of partisan politics more than this.

The increasing political polarization of recent years has seen a rise in identity politics on both ends of the political spectrum, yet the political right had spent decades decrying the identity politics used by the left only to embrace the very thing they critiqued. This shift toward performance renders the church a stage for political grandstanding rather than a space for spiritual growth. Public figures can exploit this for political gain, as seen in instances such as Donald Trump's photo op with an upside-down Bible in front of a church after the area had been cleared with tear gas and helicopters. Many who remember the insistence from Christians that "character counts" during former president Bill Clinton's sex scandal with his intern, Monica Lewinsky, felt an existential whiplash when the same people had little hesitation throwing their support behind a thrice-married man who bragged about sexual assault, owned casinos, and had been indicted for a variety of crimes. Did character really count when it was *their* power at stake?

As formative institutions, churches traditionally served as centers of spiritual guidance and moral instruction, cultivating the character of their members in alignment with Christ. This formative function naturally extended to influence believers' perspectives on social and political issues, but it did so primarily through the lens of spiritual and moral principles rather than explicit political ideologies. But increasingly, churches have been compromised by performative identity politics that form congregants into partisan voters instead of devout Christ-followers.

Still, the trend toward performative actions among certain segments of the church has had significant consequences. It risks compromising—and to many people, it has compromised—the church's ability to serve as a moral compass and prophetic witness to society, holding all political ideologies to account based on ethical principles and spiritual truths. Instead of becoming entangled in the fray of political alignment, churches ideally serve as a prophetic witness, reminding all political parties and their supporters of the moral and spiritual values that should underpin any just and compassionate society, regardless of party. The measure of success shouldn't be sheer political power but Christlikeness in all of life's stations.

Russell Moore, currently the editor-in-chief of *Christianity Today*, powerfully communicates what it is like to grow up in a religious environment that weds itself to right-wing politics in his recent book, *Losing Our Religion: An Altar Call for Evangelical America*, saying,

> Behind all of that was a dread deep within me that Christianity might just be southern culture of politics, with Jesus affixed as a hood ornament. If the gospel was just a way to mobilize voters for party bosses or to fund prostitutes and cocaine for preachers on television, that realization would be more than just an adolescent cynical awakening. It would mean, I thought, that the universe itself was a random, meaningless void in which only the fittest survive, and even then not for long. I knew there was much to love in the southern culture around me, but I could also see that just underneath the surface there was also an undercurrent of violence and hatred and seething passions of all sorts. If the gospel were just a means to propping all that up, then that would mean that these weren't aberrations, but the way the universe is, right down to the core.[9]

Jesus' kingdom is not of this world. "If my kingdom were of this world, my servants would fight, so that I wouldn't be handed over to the Jews. But as it is, my kingdom is not from here" (John 18:36). If Jesus' kingdom were of this world, then it would make sense to fight political battles against political enemies to establish him as king on earth. But that isn't how he has chosen to bring about his kingdom. Our enemies aren't political; they're spiritual (Ephesians 6:12). And we don't overcome our enemies through political power, but through the blood of the Lamb and the word of our testimony (Revelation 12:11).

This doesn't mean we can't be political. Politics is necessary for ordering a common society for people to live together. This doesn't even mean that we can't belong to one political party or the other. This is a matter of *allegiance*. Who has our highest allegiance? The state, the party, the president, or the King of kings and Lord of lords? Do we trust in the laws of humans or in the blood of the Lamb? Do we use our words to dominate others or to testify about the Risen King? The church of Jesus Christ is an outpost of Christ's kingdom. Our identity should be firmly rooted as citizens of heaven, living our lives worthy of the gospel of Christ, not partisans making arguments worthy of the party platform (Philippians 1:27).

LOSING THE PLOT

But these realities sit downstream from an even deeper issue. If these are winds and waters that erode the soil, they come from a hurricane that has swept through our churches. That hurricane is losing the plot of what the church is even supposed to be in the first place. The church has made itself the main character in God's story, displacing God as the center of gravity. The fear is that if the church doesn't stay "relevant," people will stop coming to church, the gospel will be lost, and Christianity will be over. That's why we must "move fast and break things" by "doing anything short of sin" to stay "relevant."

The performative church organizes itself around its own survival and well-being rather than the worship of God and the formation of his people. The life of the church is explainable without God. By making the church the main character of the story, God himself is inadvertently pushed out of the church and the lives of its congregants. God has left the building, and no one has realized it yet.[10]

So, where does all of this leave us? For many, the church as we know it has been compromised. The deep wells of relational connection and spiritual nourishment for us to draw on are few and far between. As the prophet Jeremiah wrote, "They have treated my people's brokenness superficially, claiming, 'Peace, peace,' when there is no peace" (Jeremiah 6:14).

We are all thirsting for living water. The church is a means of grace, a well from which we draw water in fellowship with the saints. When the well dries up and the fellowship dissolves, what is there left for those who seek God's grace? We're left with our longing for God but no place to join with his body. The thirst never goes away, even when the well is dry. It only makes sense to search for that water somewhere else. Perhaps this is why many who are deconstructing describe themselves as spiritually homeless. They set out on a journey where they are everywhere and nowhere all at once. Spiritual nomads, wandering the plains to and fro looking for water, hoping one day they'll find it.

DECONSTRUCTING SELF

THE EROSION OF OUR FAITH doesn't just happen in external institutions like the church. It also happens in our own hearts, through our innate sinful natures, which are amplified through powerful cultural narratives that we internalize and which shape our souls.[1] The effects of sin—whether it's sin done to us, by us, or around us—build up in our souls.[2] It's these *cumulative anxieties* that erode our faith when we aren't prepared for them and don't know how to handle them.

While it's easy to bemoan people's motivation to deconstruct as simply looking for ways to sin, it's much harder to admit the simple truth that is true for all believers (all *humans*, in fact)—that our sinful nature makes faith difficult. Sin is our natural state outside of God. Atheism is natural to our fallen natures; it's faith that is unnatural.[3] It's one thing to say that someone wants to leave God behind so they can sin. It's another thing to say that our sinful natures make us prone to leave God behind. We are not naturally inclined to love God, so we shouldn't be surprised when sin plays a part in someone's deconstruction one way or another.

Sometimes that plays itself out in more obvious ways than others. Maybe someone really does just want to sleep with their boyfriend or girlfriend and not feel guilty. Someone might want to embrace an alternative identity that goes against the grain of God's intended design. It might be more convenient for someone to behave immorally or unjustly than to submit to God's law of love. These are all real possibilities, but I don't think we should be surprised when people are tempted to turn their backs on God by the lust of the eyes, the lust of the flesh, and the pride of life. These aren't temptations for those whose faith is weak; these are temptations for all of us. Far from feeling self-righteous when we see someone deconstruct for these reasons, we should see an aspect of ourselves in them, understanding that we have felt the same temptations they have.

The psalmist Asaph knew this feeling well. He wrote in Psalm 73, "But as for me, my feet almost slipped; my steps nearly went astray. For I envied the arrogant; I saw prosperity in the wicked" (Psalm 73:2-3). He goes on to wonder if he had purified his heart and washed his hands in innocence for nothing (Psalm 73:13). He describes "becoming embittered" and that his "innermost being was wounded" (Psalm 73:21). These feelings don't express a lack of faith, but they do express the strength of sin. Sin tugs at our souls, beckoning us away from God. Yet God doesn't forsake us when we feel the temptation to turn from him. Asaph continues, "My flesh and my strength may fail, but God is the strength of my heart, my portion forever" (Psalm 73:26).

But other times, no discernible sinful desire pulls us away from God. It is just the reality of our fallen nature itself. We see reality only through a dark glass (1 Corinthians 13:12). We have belief mixed with unbelief (Mark 9:24). We mistake God's hiddenness for his rejection (Psalm 88:14). In short, we're human. Part and parcel of being human on this side of eternity is wrestling with the sin that pulls us away from God until we're finally delivered, one degree of glory to the next (2 Corinthians 3:18). As Augustine wrote in *Confessions*, "If there were as many different natures in us as there are conflicting wills, we should have a great many more natures than merely two."[4] When faith in God isn't the natural warp and woof of the human soul as it's marred by sin, we should expect its gradual transformation to Christlikeness to be a difficult process that is often difficult to endure.

OUR PERFORMATIVE IDENTITIES

Our individual selves—along with our sinful natures—don't exist in isolation. They exist in relationship with others and the broader world around us. They're shaped not only by the Spirit of God and our own rational faculties, but by the stories—the cultural narratives—that we absorb both consciously and subconsciously.[5] While there are many narratives that shape us, it's not an exaggeration to say the most powerful narrative that erodes the soil of our hearts is that of individualism.

Jean Twenge writes in her groundbreaking book *Generations*,

> Why is religion less popular with Millennials? In short, because it is not compatible with individualism—and individualism is Millennials' core value above all else. Individualism promotes focusing on the self and finding your own way, and religion by definition promotes focusing on things larger than the self and following certain rules. One Millennial said of her beliefs, "[W]hatever you feel, it's personal. Everybody has their own idea of God and what God is. . . . You have your own personal beliefs of what's acceptable for you and what's right for you personally." Another described leaving his church because "I was not being encouraged to think for myself. [Religious rules are] literally, 'This is black. This is white. Do this. Don't do that.' And I can't hang with that."[6]

Jesus saves us into a community—the church, the family of God, his body. But our culture has separated us from one another, telling us that *we* are what we should value most. And our society is set up to reinforce that narrative. We see our own reflection in black mirrors more than we see the eyes of others. We trust therapists with our problems more than friends or family. We believe YouTubers, podcasters, and influencers more than we believe our pastors, professors, and other experts. We eschew marriage and children for a life free from inhibitions so we can express our true selves to the world. We are performers, our identity is the script, and the whole world is our stage.

Alan Noble, in his book *You Are Not Your Own,* powerfully communicates how this way of being dehumanizes us and erodes our souls. The primary narrative told by the world of expressive individualism is "I am my own and I belong to myself." This narrative of self-belonging stands in stark contrast to the foundational question of the Heidelberg Catechism, "What is our only hope in life and death? That I am not my own, but belong—body and soul, in life and in death—to my faithful Savior, Jesus Christ." Noble proposes that our society is deeply embedded in this self-focused narrative and, consequently, we carry the Responsibilities of Self-Belonging. These responsibilities include the obligation to (1) justify our existence, (2) create an identity, (3) discover meaning, (4) choose values, and (5) find a place of belonging.[7] We're expected to do all of this on our own.

When we are our own and belong to ourselves, we are solely responsible for shaping these aspects of our lives. This responsibility turns us inward to search for answers within ourselves, a search with no source or guide. Nothing captures this aimlessness better than Taylor Swift's NYU commencement speech in 2022, when she said, "I know it can be really overwhelming figuring out who to be, and when. Who you are now and how to act in order to get where you want to go. I have some good news: It's totally up to you. I also have some terrifying news: It's totally up to you."[8] Overwhelming and terrifying, indeed.

In our secular age, it's up to us to figure out who we are, what our purpose is, and how to do something to subjectively prove our worth to ourselves and to others. If anyone tries to tell you who you should be, just shake it off. Are we surprised that everyone is burned out? Is it any wonder that we now have multiple generations struggling with depression, anxiety, and suicide?[9] When the weight of your purpose rests on your own shoulders, you'll break under the pressure of other people's expectations.

This story of self-belonging puts us at odds with others whose discovered answers diverge from our own. In the absence of an agreed-upon narrative for humanity, we find ourselves in competition, a perpetual struggle for the survival of the fittest.[10] The pressure of finding and expressing yourself is exhausting. We are constantly under pressure to affirm the truth of the identity we've settled on, and the only way to do so is by performing our identities for others, seeking their affirmation.[11] To be more "authentic," we resort to *technique*, always tweaking our life to become the best possible version of ourselves.[12]

Alan Noble continues,

> Implicit in our society is the promise that you can become a fully realized human if you:
>
> 1. Accept that you are your own and belong completely to yourself.
>
> 2. Work every day to discover and express yourself.
>
> 3. Use all of the techniques and methods perfected by society to improve your life and conquer your obstacles.[13]

This path inevitably leads us to one of two outcomes: affirmation or resignation. Affirmation involves ceaselessly pursuing achievement, refining techniques, and garnering rewards and accolades to validate our self-created identities. Resignation, on the other hand, is a total withdrawal from the race, not toward something superior like belonging to Christ, but surrendering in shame as someone who failed to find their "authentic" self.[14]

If our society is designed around an inhuman anthropology that encourages us to search inward for ourselves instead of looking outward to Christ, then we are not being shaped by God but instead are performing our identities for each other. This perpetual performance erodes our humanity as we consistently seek affirmation from others that is already ours in Christ, which leads to either forcefully imposing our identities on others or resigning from the societal rat race in shame and despair. Either way, there seems to be no escape from this cycle. It's another treadmill of trying harder that gridlocks our imagination.

By way of eroding our identity, our faith is eroded as well. We no longer receive an identity from God that we accept and shape our life around. Now we create our own identities, scripts for our life, and narratives of reality, and we live by those instead.[15] God isn't our highest authority for our sense of self, our purpose, and our meaning; we are.

In her book *Self-Made: Creating Our Identities from Da Vinci to the Kardashians*, Tara Isabella Burton writes, "We have turned our backs on the idea of a creator-God, out there, and instead placed God within us—more specifically, within the numinous force of our own desires. Our obsession with self-creation is also an obsession with the idea that we have the power that we once believed God did: to remake ourselves and our realities, not in the image of God but in that of our own desires."[16]

SALVATION BY THERAPY ALONE

The pressure of self-belonging, finding our "true self," and keeping up appearances is exhausting. How do we know if we have accomplished it? Which true self do we need to stay true to when we feel conflicted? If we can't find our true self, then we might as well have failed to be human.[17] Staying true to yourself comes at the high cost of being entirely responsible for defining your identity apart from others.

This, of course, is impossible. Our identities are unmistakably intertwined with our relationships with others. My identity isn't something that I project onto others, it's something that is *recognized* by others. My identity is reflected back to me in my relationships. I can't force anything on them. Who they perceive me to be is an essential part of my identity. If I don't like how people perceive me, I can't change that simply by declaring a different identity and changing external appearances; I have to change my *character*.

When you are in charge of defining your identity apart from God, all you have left is *technique*. You're stuck on a constant treadmill of trying harder, self-optimization, and performing for others' validation. You can do this for a while, but you can't do it long before you burn out. We demand a way out. We need salvation from our-selves and the crushing responsibilities that self-belonging brings with it.

So, for many today, the place to turn to for relief is therapy. Therapy allows us to rehabilitate ourselves from the burdens of self-belonging so we can continue to perform. More than that, it becomes its own play for us to act in.

The rise of therapy and the destigmatization of mental health issues are, in many ways, good things. It is crucial that individuals are given the ability to process and heal from their traumas and mental health conditions without shame or stigma. However, the challenge lies in the proliferation of "therapy speak"—a phenomenon where therapeutic language seeps into everyday dialogue, reducing its potency, claiming undue authority, and broadly applying its prin-ciples to the general public.[18]

Therapy easily transitions from a specialized psychological service intended to aid the individual into a broad sociological prescription aimed at reforming society. This raises the concern that therapy speak can act as a façade for genuine systemic societal problems by placing the responsibility of change onto the individual.

This isn't to critique professional therapists providing essential ser-vices or those seeking therapy, but rather the permeation of therapy speak into our culture, turning it into a pseudoreligious phenomenon.

Some have drawn an intriguing parallel between therapy and re-ligion, arguing that therapy has replaced the function that religion used to play in our society. Therapy has become the new confession, self-affirming mantras have replaced prayers, communities with the same diagnosis have supplanted church groups, and self-actualization has taken the place of salvation.[19]

Yet, therapy's focus on self-improvement diverges from religion's emphasis on communal relationships and spirituality. It offers no ul-timate salvation from personal struggles. The only promise therapy provides is the relentless task of "doing the work," leaving individuals on an incessant treadmill of technique.

The persistent pursuit of self-improvement is not only emotionally draining but also economically taxing. Therapy is a luxury that many cannot afford. Prescribing it as a panacea for societal problems only accentuates the class divide where the well-off can "do the work" and the poor are left stuck in their trauma.

The proliferation of therapy speak has led to a surge in therapeutic social media influencers offering diluted—even entirely misguided—advice. These influencers often profit from the trauma and mental health struggles of their less affluent followers through ad revenue and online course sales. Ironically, this can exacerbate mental health issues rather than alleviate them. Doctors and psychologists are beginning to warn about the dangers of self-diagnosing mental health disorders based on social media content.[20]

Therapy is not all bad. Therapy can be good. The challenge lies in being able to tell the difference between the good things that help us and the vitally necessary things that sustain us. Someone might need therapy coupled with community support, medication alongside spiritual practices, introspection about trauma with emotional resilience building, and self-care combined with responsibilities that serve others. Above all, we all need grace, without which we will all be run ragged on the treadmill of trying harder.

Therapy, mental health awareness, and medication have made significant strides in recent years, and this progress shouldn't be reversed. However, it's equally essential to ensure we don't lose sight of other crucial aspects of our personhood and not seek salvation in something that can't save us.

DEVICES OF DECONSTRUCTION

Our digital devices and the proliferation of social media only add fuel to this fire as they remove us from our local, embodied relationships and institutions and project our curated identities for a watching audience. Social media is the ultimate performance machine, extracting our personalities as products and counterfeiting our institutions by shaping us in invisible molds we didn't consciously consent to. My own deconstruction story is an example of this at work.

YouTube sparked my deconstruction. Being an only child who had experienced substantial suffering, hoping to find answers, I consumed a huge amount of digital content to help make sense of my experiences and my faith instead of spending time with friends or working on school assignments.

An encounter with one of the original YouTube deconversion stories pushed me into the throes of deconstruction. One by one, the narrator knocked out the pillars of my faith until it had nothing to stand on. Instead of going to my pastor for guidance, I turned to content creators online. Podcasts like *The Liturgists* further catalyzed my process. The digital world provided the illusion of spiritual nourishment I thought I needed.

Our media diets have the power to form and deform our faith. And the algorithms that feed us our content diet aren't neutral. They know exactly what questions we're asking, what life stage we're in, what fears we have, where we live, and who on the internet is speaking to those things.

Every post you make, every like, every search, every time you linger for five seconds instead of two on a post, the algorithm registers your interest and feeds you more content like it. The doubts in our hearts are expressed through the movement of our fingertips, and nothing we do on our screens is hidden from the algorithm. Our vulnerabilities are opportunities for rabbit holes of content we didn't know existed to open like trapdoors under our feet.

Social media is a spiritual distortion zone. It acts as a spiritual and cognitive distortion machine that warps our view of reality and bends our will away from God. It's the systematic, corporately incentivized inversion of Romans 12:1–2. Instead of our minds being renewed by the Spirit of Christ, they're shaped by algorithmically curated delivery of the particular patterns of the world that best play to our unsanctified desires. They beckon us into conformity with the world by drawing our hearts and minds away from God.

In Andy Crouch's book *The Life We're Looking For*, he distinguishes between devices and instruments.[21] Devices and instruments alike are akin to magic in that they expand our capacities and reduce our burdens. Bicycles, for instance, allow us to travel great distances with less effort and time than walking or running. Pianos allow us to play music that we couldn't with our voices alone. These are instruments in that they expand our capacities and reduce our burdens but also still require something from the user. You can't simply sit down at a piano one day and learn to play like Beethoven. You have to *become the kind of person* that can play the piano like Beethoven. With great power comes great responsibility, as Uncle Ben famously told Spider-Man.

But devices are different. They maximize the distance between power and character. Devices greatly expand capabilities while greatly reducing burdens. This is what computers and smartphones do. We have instant access to nearly limitless knowledge and the ability to create almost anything we want, and all we have to do is tap our fingers a few times to conjure it—whatever it is—on demand.

Crouch talks about how instruments and devices both make two promises to us:

- "Now you'll be able to . . ."
- "You'll no longer have to . . ."[22]

These are wonderful uses of technology. But the wider the gap between the ability needed to use it and the power it gives you, there are two other promises that devices make that are unintended consequences of the first two promises. They are

- "You'll no longer be able to . . ."
- "Now you'll have to . . ."

In other words, while devices might give us expanded capabilities and reduced burdens, they also give us "restricted capabilities and enforced burdens."[23] You will be able to do more with less than before, but you'll also *have* to do certain things within new limits that you didn't have before. Our devices are both blessings and curses.

What does this mean for our faith when we have infinite access to spiritual content? What do we gain, and what do we lose when devices become our primary mediator for spiritual content and facilitator of discipleship? It might look something like this:

- *Now you'll be able to* access spiritual content from anywhere for free.
- *You'll no longer have to* pay for an expensive seminary education or rely solely on your local pastor for good teaching and instruction in the faith.
- *You'll no longer be able to* easily discern the difference between trusted, credible voices and those who are ill-informed or malicious.
- *Now you'll have to* choose who to trust more: your local church or the content you consume.

The ability to access quality spiritual content for free is an incredible innovation. Much like the printing press before it, it releases the riches of the faith from the spiritual elite and provides access to the priesthood of believers. For those who are in churches that are too small (or performative) to resource their people well, there's an opportunity to learn from others anywhere in the world.

But this has also diminished our capacity to trust our pastors and communities. Alternative facts don't just exist in the political sphere, but also in the religious sphere. Every heresy has a Bible verse, and now those heresies are being fed as novelties to the faith curious and institutionally skeptical on TikTok, Instagram, Facebook, and Twitter. The digital liturgies of scrolling, swiping, liking, posting, and viewing have the power to transform our minds. When the internet becomes the chief architect of our plausibility structures, we have quite literally lost touch with reality, as we now view the world primarily through the six-inch screen in our hands rather than our real-life, flesh-and-blood relationships.

That leaves us with a choice. Who do we trust more: Our local church or the content that we consume? Social media has become the counterfeit institution we turn to when we feel uncomfortable in our physical institutions.[24] Many times, the content that we consume rightly exposes abuse in the church. However, the media we consume isn't the liberation we think it is. It will rapture us out of our communities, our place, and our bodies, and into cyberspace, leaving us without the very things that bring meaning to our lives. The answer isn't to leave our communities for the safe haven of social media; it is to embed ourselves into our local communities *more*.

THE LONELINESS CRISIS

With all of this in mind, it shouldn't surprise us that in 2023, the US Surgeon General announced that we are experiencing an epidemic of loneliness. The report read,

> Loneliness is far more than just a bad feeling—it harms both individual and societal health. . . . Given the profound consequences of loneliness and isolation, we have an opportunity, and an obligation, to make the same investments in addressing social connection that we have made in addressing tobacco use, obesity, and the addiction crisis. This Surgeon General's Advisory shows us how to build more connected lives and a more connected society.
>
> If we fail to do so, we will pay an ever-increasing price in the form of our individual and collective health and well-being. And we will continue to splinter and divide until we can no longer stand as a community or a country. Instead of coming together to take on the great challenges before us, we will further retreat to our corners—angry, sick, and alone.[25]

We're starved for connection but afraid to reach out for it. We think social media and therapy can cure our ills when what we need is a community that cares for us and friends that we can trust. Our quest for self-expression and carrying the responsibilities of self-belonging is crushing us. Our values are upside down. Instead of seeking to express ourselves, we're meant to care for others. Instead of trying to find our true selves, we're meant to take responsibility for our neighbor.

Right now, our culture is putting a Band-Aid on a gunshot wound, in the form of loose communities around things like self-care, yoga, vague spiritualism, astrology, running clubs, CrossFit, politics, activism, and more. Some of these are better than others, but what is needed is deep connections, relationships, and the communal support that only the church can provide.[26]

Who is going to cry with you after a death in the family? Who will bring you meals after your child is born? Who will introduce you to a man or woman of character with the potential for marriage? Who can you trust to confess your sins to and help you grow into the image of Christ? Can others depend on you for those things? Are you so embedded in a community that your presence makes a difference in others' lives? Would you be noticed if you were gone?

The Catholic writer Ronald Rolheiser says,

> Part of the very essence of Christianity is to be together in a concrete community, with all the real human faults that are there and the tensions that this will bring. Spirituality, for the Christian, can never be an individualistic quest, the pursuit of God outside of community, family, and church. The God of the incarnation tells us that anyone who says that he or she loves an invisible God in heaven and is unwilling to deal with a visible neighbor on earth is a liar since no one can love a God who cannot be seen if he or she cannot love a neighbor who can be seen.[27]

Not only do we need people to take responsibility for our well-being, but it's also incumbent on us to take responsibility for the well-being of others. It's one thing to talk about values like compassion, diversity, inclusion, vulnerability, and justice. It's another thing to live them out.

How can you live them out except in community? How can you act on your values except in meaningful, thick relationships with others? The very things that bring meaning to our lives don't happen alone; they happen with others in community. And our community is always mediated by an institution, whether it be a bar, a dining table, or a church. Why would you not organize your life in a community of mutual care?

Individualism is killing us, and it's killing our faith. Good, genuine relationships and community are possible. It requires risk, commitment, time, and work, but it will lead to a richer, more meaningful life and faith. Church shouldn't be an afterthought in our lives. It should be one of our most important priorities—not to consume religious goods and services, but to embody the life of Christ, loving God and loving neighbor, in real flesh-and-blood relationships.

Behind this vision for community is a dark shadow that is lurking, a shadow we've already explored in chapter five. Not all churches are places where this is possible. Many have been compromised, and instead of allowing for a community like this to flourish, they exploit the community, using it for their own performance and squashing these kinds of relationships. That doesn't mean this vision of community is impossible, it just means we need to reconstruct our churches. That's something we will explore in a future chapter.

We are made of dust, not code. Content and therapy may supplement what we lack from our physical community, but it can never fill the wells that we drink from for meaning. We need church, the bread of the Word, the living water of Christ, and the fellowship of the Spirit in prayer. We must walk with trusted, wise guides in a community of others who know us as real people, believing they will help us find the light when everything seems dark.

My hope is that we catch the vision—the *need*—for healthy relationships, community, and churches. If we understand the necessity of this kind of community, we will search it out high and low, turning over every rock until we find it. Our *self* wouldn't stand a chance without it.

THE ENDS OF
DECONSTRUCTION

IT'S COMMON TO HEAR PEOPLE SAY that the goal of deconstruction should be reconstructing something better in its place. I have said that in the past, and many well-meaning, sincere ministers and leaders have said similar things as well.[1] From a certain perspective, it makes complete sense. Why would you deconstruct something if you weren't planning on reconstructing something else?

I've heard people say, "Deconstruction without reconstruction is just destruction."[2] The implication is that if someone is in the midst of deconstruction without any intention to reconstruct their faith, then they are simply destructive individuals who have no concern for the truth. I'm sympathetic to why someone would feel this way, but it simply isn't a helpful way to frame it.

Deconstruction is a *crisis*. Instead of reconstruction being the *goal* of deconstruction, it might be more accurate to say that reconstruction is the inevitable *outcome* of deconstruction. *What* is reconstructed is anything but inevitable, but something *must* be reconstructed. Everyone reconstructs. It's impossible not to. If we lived in a perpetual state of deconstruction with nothing to fill its place, we would fall apart. You can only tear down so much before the crisis becomes so great that you are forced into reconstruction just to find a balm for the pain. You might be grasping at straws, but it's better than the rubble you've been standing in.

This is why in my definition of deconstruction, I say that deconstruction is a crisis of faith "that settles in a faith that is different from before." For some, that might sound like I mean reconstructing a stronger faith than the one you deconstructed. That is certainly a possibility, and it is the desired outcome of this book. However, someone else might read that and think, "What do you mean 'faith'? I don't have faith! I don't believe anything anymore." And that, too, is a potential outcome, but even that response isn't quite accurate. Everyone has faith. A third person might read that and nod their head, thinking about how much their beliefs have changed and look nothing like what they used to. They're no longer Christians—or at least not anything like the way they used to think about Christians—but they do consider themselves spiritual and "in touch with the Divine." It just looks completely different from before.

These three ways of responding to that definition get at a crucial distinction: while deconstruction inevitably leads to reconstruction, *there is no inevitable outcome of reconstruction*. Everyone reconstructs, but not everyone reconstructs the same thing. As you can imagine, this is scary for everyone involved. The person deconstructing has no idea if they will be a Christian by the end of it or not. Those who know and love the person deconstructing are anxious, wondering if they're still going to be a Christian or not. If that scares you, welcome to the experience of deconstruction. It's terrifying.

WORLDS FALLING APART

Whether we're conscious of it or not, all of us form our beliefs through a combination of rational, experiential, and social means.[3] If something doesn't make some level of rational sense to us, we'll start to feel the cognitive dissonance that something is missing. If something directly contradicts our lived experience, we're going to be far more skeptical of its validity. If no one around us believes what we believe, the chances that we can maintain belief are slim.

Our beliefs reflect our social aspirations more than we would like to admit. If we start to feel ostracized by or different from the group we currently belong to, we might begin to question the beliefs that we share with them. "If they believe that, and I don't feel like I belong, maybe I *don't* believe that." The truth of the belief is understood in relation to the strength of the social connection. The way our faith is formed is far more complex than the rational decisions we make. We might think we understand how we came to believe what we believe, but we might only be grasping a part of the whole.

Everyone has faith in something. We swim like fish in cultural waters every day of our lives, unaware of the water because it is all we know.[4] The way we view everything—ourselves, family, God, politics, the economy, what food is good, what movies we like, education, race, gender, and so on—is shaped by the cultural water we swim in. In his book *Biblical Critical Theory*, Christopher Watkin calls this water "Worlds."

Worlds are "a set of particular figures that give a rhythm to the space, time, ideas, reality, behavior, and relationships in a particular sphere of life, among a particular community, or in a particular artist's work, giving them a distinct style."[5] The "world" through which we experience and understand life is really the combination of many different forces that all give a different shade and color to the lenses we see through. These forces are what Watkin calls "figures." These figures are what shape the plausibility structures that we see through to determine what could be true and not true. Watkin lists several different figures that influence us:

- language, ideas, and stories (words, metaphors, and concepts)
- time and space (how we structure our time and view our physical space)
- the structure of reality (is the world purely natural, or is there the possibility of the supernatural?)
- behavior (working, resting, eating, shopping, looking at your phone, and so on)

- relationships (family, friends, church, school, nation, community, and so on)
- objects (homes, phones, TVs, cars, cities, and so on)

These figures exist independently of us and exert their force on us without our conscious consent and are different for every person depending on their location in culture. The less aware of them we are, the more this is true. But being aware of them doesn't mean they don't affect us. There is no factory default setting for humans. We're not blank slates. Our view of the world is influenced by the confluence of all these figures, and we are constantly being reconfigured every time we encounter something new. And our figures are made up of things that are provable (the things we can see, hear, and touch) and things that aren't provable at all (like love, friendship, hope, and human rights).

It might not change us dramatically, but it does reconfigure us ever so slightly just by adding one layer of difference to what we knew before. Some things we encounter might reconfigure us so radically that our old figures stop working as well as they did before. That is when we begin to actively look for ways to reconfigure our whole "World," so we can make more sense of reality than we were previously able to.

The way new figures help us make sense of reality is when they tell a better, more congruent story than our old figures, which allows us to live with more harmony and less dissonance. When someone is deconstructing their faith, their "World" is being reconfigured because the figures they had in their faith community no longer make sense of reality. Either they discovered a fundamental flaw in a figure they held, were exposed to other figures that told a better story than their Christian figures, or both. If someone says that deconstruction felt like their "world was falling apart," that's because it was. Literally.

When someone's world falls apart, it is simultaneously reconfigured by any number of different influences. This reconfiguration of worlds is what we're talking about when we talk about reconstruction. It's more than simply finding new theological beliefs. It's reconstructing an entire world, a new reality in every aspect of our lives. Who we are on the other side will not be the same person we were before.

So, if reconstruction is a reconfiguration of our worlds and has no inevitable outcome, what are the *potential* outcomes of reconstruction? While the possibilities are as endless as there are individuals, we can simplify and summarize them in three general categories: *replace, remix,* or *renew.*

It's worth noting that—like everything else that we've discussed so far in this book—there are no clean lines when it comes to these things. Even while I break these possibilities down into categories, you might know people who resemble parts of two or three categories or move between them at different times. That's because we are complex beings and our stories rarely fit into neat boxes. The following categories are meant to be a simplified way of understanding some general landing spots.

REPLACING FAITH

The first potential outcome is that you will replace your faith in Christ with faith in something else. This goes back to the idea that it's impossible to release faith entirely, but it is possible to replace it. These are people who leave behind Christianity entirely. They no longer claim to follow Jesus. They no longer attend church. They have completely shed the veneer of Christianity. The two primary things that people replace their faith with are intellectualism and intuition.

Intellectualism. These are the people who look to data and statistics for their beliefs. "Follow the science!" is their mantra. Their quest for an empirically provable worldview means they reject claims that can't be backed up by verifiable evidence. For them, the scientific method is the standard by which all truth claims need to be measured.

When the resurrection can't be proved in a scientifically verifiable way, they reject the claim. The same is true for all other theological claims. Miracles, the afterlife, inspiration of the Bible, the existence of God. None of these can be proved in the same way that we can prove gravity exists. That doesn't mean there aren't valid reasons for believing them, but the Intellectualist won't be convinced until empirical evidence can be produced.

The Intellectualist exists entirely in what philosopher Charles Taylor calls "the immanent frame." It's the idea that there is nothing transcendent, nothing greater than us. They live in a closed world, not open to the possibility of anything beyond what we can observe.

The problem is that these people often hold beliefs that they can't prove: things like human rights, the goodness of kindness and compassion, and the necessity of helping the poor. There is nothing scientifically provable about the goodness of these beliefs. So, they are forced to find reasons why they hold them. They might say that the beliefs are good because they are evolutionarily beneficial to our species, so we collectively agreed that they are good. Our feeling of love is nothing more than a chemical reaction in our brains that pushes us toward reproduction for the propagation of the species. Even our highest values are regarded in immanent, scientific terms. Yet they can't prove that they actually exist in any meaningful way.

Ben Gibbard, singer of the legendary indie band Death Cab for Cutie, sings in their haunting song "St. Peter's Cathedral," "There's nothing past this," over and over again for two minutes and twenty-three seconds straight, almost convincing himself that it's true. This is the driving belief of the one who leaves their faith for pure intellectualism.

Intuition. The second way people replace their faith is through intuition. This is the opposite of intellectualism. Instead of needing data for their beliefs, they don't need anything other than their own intuition.[6] It's vibes all the way down.

In 2020, popular YouTube comedy duo Rhett and Link shared their stories of deconstruction with their audience of over 5.5 million subscribers.[7] Every year since, they've done videos providing updates on their spiritual journey. In one of their follow-up videos, Link says, "My spiritual practice is resolving to know nothing."[8] This is the essence of Intuitionism. God, church, and religion are all but gone from their minds. It's not something they think about. Instead, they simply try to follow their hearts, be themselves, and do what seems right to them—as long as it doesn't hurt anyone.

They've replaced their spiritual practices with self-care practices, and churchgoing with community involvement or political activism. They are trying to make the best life for themselves and those around them without the confines of religion. They may not be particularly hostile to it, but it's just not part of their lives anymore. The moral compass of their life has shifted from external religion to internal intuition. Guided by their own thoughts and feelings, they have left Christianity behind for the religion of self.

REMIXING FAITH

The next group of people haven't left Christianity behind entirely, at least not in their minds. By "remixing," I mean mixing Christianity with something else that is inherently opposed to Christianity. It retains some resemblance to Christianity, but it's been diluted and changed so that it's no longer recognizable as the historic Christian faith.

These folks might still call themselves Christian or are at least indifferent about the term. They have for sure left anything resembling evangelicalism. Most people aren't replacing their faith entirely. They're remixing it. Many of these are the folks who—along with those who follow their intuition—would say that they are "spiritual, not religious," which is about 27 percent of Americans, according to a 2017 Pew study.[9] The two primary ways that people remix their faith are with ideology and idolatry.

Ideology. Some people remix their faith with ideology. This isn't just a problem in deconstruction circles. Many on the conservative right have remixed their faith with nationalism to the point that it's no longer Christian. I don't want this to seem like it's only a temptation to the left. It isn't.

That said, for most people who grew up in conservative evangelical environments and are now deconstructing, the tendency is to throw out their conservative values and embrace progressive values in their place. If they were pro-life before, now they're pro-choice. If they accepted a traditional view of sexuality before, now they are LGBTQ+ affirming. This isn't to say that you can't hold to some progressive policy positions and be a Christian. The problem is when these views become what it *means* to be a Christian.

It's a mirror image of conservative fundamentalism. Progressive policies become the new litmus test of faithfulness. If you aren't LGBTQ+ affirming, then you aren't loving, and you aren't a real Christian. If you aren't pro-choice, you hate women, and you aren't a real Christian. If you're pro-capitalism, you hate the poor, and—you guessed it—you aren't a real Christian. It's the same works-based burdens that fundamentalists placed on them when they were younger, just in the opposite direction.

Idolatry. The next way people remix their faith is through idolatry. This might take more nebulous forms, such as the "idols of the heart"—money, sex, status, and power. They might turn them*selves* into an idol and pursue all the pleasure and power possible. But I also mean *actual* idolatry; remixing the Christian faith with other religions and other gods—a modern-day violation of the first commandment: "Have no other gods before me."

Tara Isabella Burton writes, "These are the 'religious hybrids': People who say they belong to a given religion, and believe or practice a portion of it. But they also feel free to disregard elements that don't necessarily suit them, or to supplement their official practice with spiritual or ritualistic elements, not to mention beliefs, from other traditions."[10]

The primary way this happens is by reinterpreting Christian words to mean things that aren't Christian. *The Liturgists* dedicated an entire season of their podcast to this project. They explicitly attempted to redefine words such as *Trinity, salvation, Satan, heaven, hell, resurrection*, *Jesus*, and *sin* to align more with a non-dual, panentheistic view of the universe.

You see this with writers such as Richard Rohr in his book *The Universal Christ,* where he defines Christ as "the indwelling of the Divine Presence in everyone and everything since the beginning of time as we know it."[11] He separates Jesus and "the Christ" into two distinct entities in a way that has never been recognized by the historic church or the New Testament writers. In fact, it was condemned as the heresy of Nestorianism at the Council of Ephesus in AD 431 and again at the Council of Chalcedon in 451. Rohr mentions once that the word *Christ* comes from the Hebrew word for "Messiah," which means "Anointed One," and then goes on to interpret that as meaning *everything* is anointed.[12] That is not how the biblical authors, whose minds were soaked in the Old Testament, understood the word "Christ."

It shouldn't be surprising that, at some point or another, many people move through this to the point of dropping the pretense of spirituality entirely. As pastor and author Andrew Wilson writes, "It is hard to promote or proscribe certain behavior if you think your moral framework is merely a useful fiction."[13]

Reinterpreting Christian words apart from their historical meanings and in light of other religious traditions is key to remixing Christianity. This is how you end up with Christian Buddhists or Christians incorporating Hindu spirituality into their practice. As Jesus said, "No one can serve two masters, since either he will hate one and love the other, or he will be devoted to one and despise the other. You cannot serve both God and . . ." (Matthew 6:24). How do you finish that sentence? The NIV translates it as "money." A more literal translation is "Mammon," who was the god of money. Jesus literally named another god, a rival god of Yahweh's. Jesus was warning his listeners about the dangers of remixing their faith with other gods. You cannot serve both Yahweh and Mammon. You cannot serve both Jesus and another god. It's impossible. One will make you turn on the other. A house divided against itself cannot stand.

RENEWING FAITH

The final potential outcome of deconstruction is a renewed faith. This is when someone pushes through The Wall of deconstruction and comes out the other side with their faith in Jesus stronger than before. It doesn't mean all their questions are answered, or all of their doubts are relieved. No, the person who has gone through deconstruction isn't going to be fooled into thinking they need to have perfect certainty about much anymore. What they have instead is trust: a *settled confidence.* They are confident in who Jesus is, confident in the good news of the gospel, confident that God will bring to completion the work that he started in them, and they have surrendered to his will (Philippians 1:5-7).

It's impossible to emphasize this enough: a renewed faith doesn't come from answering every question, it doesn't come from doing all the right things, it doesn't come from saying just the right words. It comes when the Holy Spirit illuminates the eyes of their heart to the beauty of Jesus in the gospel.

In his book *Reappearing Church,* Mark Sayers wrote that renewal is, "The refreshment, release, and advancement that individuals, groups, and churches experience when they are realigned with God's presence"[14] and that "renewal follows periods of crisis, change, and transition."[15] There's that word, *crisis,* again. A radical transformation happens when someone is realigned with God's presence. Instead of the worry and anxiety that come with wondering if their faith is strong enough, they feel refreshed by God's love and released from their worries. Confidence takes over as they learn to relax and rest in God, knowing that he holds them and that, truly, he always has.

Illumination. Remember our ground-zero passage for deconstruction in 1 Corinthians 3? Reading the chapter just before it, 1 Corinthians 2, became a pivotal moment in my own reconstruction.

If 1 Corinthians 3 is ground zero for how I think about deconstruction, 1 Corinthians 2 is ground zero for how I think about illumination in the process of reconstruction.

> Now God has revealed these things to us by the Spirit, since the Spirit searches everything, even the depths of God. For who knows a person's thoughts except his spirit within him? In the same way, no one knows the thoughts of God except the Spirit of God. Now we have not received the spirit of the world, but the Spirit who comes from God, so that we may understand what has been freely given to us by God. (1 Corinthians 2:10-12)

The only reason we understand the mysteries of God is that God has given us his Spirit, and the Spirit reveals "what has been freely given to us." God has revealed the mystery of himself to us and has illuminated that knowledge to us by his Spirit. This is the only way someone can come to know God. God himself must give them his Spirit and illuminate their hearts and minds.

There can be the temptation when reconstructing your faith to take credit for your reconstruction. After all the hard work, research, emotional processing, conversations, debates, and struggle to find God when he feels so far away, when you finally find him, it's understandable to say, "at last, I have found God!" And there certainly is the act of seeking God involved. David writes in Psalm 9:10, "Those who know your name trust in you because you have not abandoned those who seek you, Lord." But while we seek to find God, we cannot forget his faithfulness to not abandon us.

It's God's grace in our lives that he allows us to "seek the Lord while he may be found; call on him while he is near" (Isaiah 55:6). It seems that even Paul reminds himself of this truth when he writes in Galatians 4:9, "But now, since you know God, or rather have become known by God." And again, in Philippians 3:12 when Paul says that he makes "every effort to take hold of [Christ] because I also have been taken hold of by Christ Jesus."

All our efforts to find God are only possible because God takes hold of us first and allows himself to be found by us. Reconstruction is far more a process of cooperating with God, who has called us to himself, than it is reasoning our way to the knowledge of the Infinite One. A thriving faith can't be reconstructed without trust that there is a God to be known. There's no safe landing without a leap of faith first.

As we move on to talking about reconstruction, it will be tempting to turn the following chapters into a formula. Do this and this, and that, and voilà, their faith has been reconstructed! But that's simply not how the spiritual life works. That's not how God works. What we want to do is offer ourselves as vessels for God to use in the lives of those who are searching for him. Be prepared to have conversations, pray, and love them well. But this is a process that is in God's hands, not ours.

There's no program, paradigm, training, or technique that can warm someone's heart to the love of God without him opening their eyes to see him first. But I believe God is faithful to honor those who earnestly seek him with humble and trusting hearts. As God promised his people Israel when they were going into exile, "You will seek me and find me when you search for me with all your heart" (Jeremiah 29:13). We are entirely and utterly dependent on him to illuminate his mysteries. And the good news is that he still does this.

PART 2

RECONSTRUCT

RECONSTRUCTING RELATIONSHIPS

ONE OF THE MOST FAMOUS and influential Christians to ever live left the faith of his childhood. Today, he's a saint. His name is Augustine of Hippo.

Saint Augustine was the bishop of Hippo who lived in North Africa in the late fourth and early fifth centuries AD. Raised by a Christian mother and a pagan father, Augustine left the Christian faith at eighteen years old—just a year after his father passed away—to join a rival faith called Manichaeism.[1] Augustine's departure from the faith deeply grieved his mother, Monica. Augustine records in his *Confessions* that his mother "wept to [God] for me, shedding more tears for my spiritual death than other mothers shed for the bodily death of a son."[2]

I imagine the way Monica felt for her son is how many parents, siblings, friends, and pastors feel for those they love who are deconstructing their faith. Maybe they've left the faith entirely or maybe they're just wrestling with it, unsure of what to make of everything. But either way, the difficulty of watching someone you care about deconstruct their faith is its own grieving process. All you wish is for them to find peace with God, comfort in their souls, and a joyous life lived in God's light. Yet that simply isn't the season they find themselves in. They're wrestling with God in the dark night of the soul, sometimes holding on for dear life and other times letting go and seeing what else the world has to offer. We wish we could just snap our fingers or say the right words and make everything right for them. But we can't. What can we do?

In *Confessions*, Augustine tells a story of a time when his mother went to a priest who had himself grown up as a Manichee and had later become a Christian. She asked the priest to talk with Augustine to "refute [his] errors, drive the evil out of [his] mind, and replace it with good." Surprisingly, the priest refused to speak with Augustine, no matter how much Monica insisted. Why wouldn't the priest meet with him? Augustine records his reason, "He told her that I was still unripe for instruction . . . brimming over with the novelty of the heresy. . . . 'Leave him alone,' he said. 'Just pray to God for him. From his own reading he will discover his mistakes and the depth of his profanity.'"[3] What did this priest know that Monica didn't know?

The priest knew that neither he, nor Monica, nor any other human had the power to save Augustine. Not because there was nothing he could do to show Augustine a different way of being a Christian, or have good conversations where he introduced ideas from a different perspective, or that his presence in his life wouldn't have any effect on his faith. All of those things were true.

The reason that the priest couldn't save Augustine is the same reason that you or I can't save anyone: We're not God. We have no control over anyone's salvation. Only God does. God, in his sovereignty, calls people to himself as he sees fit and when he sees fit. It's God's power that saves, not ours. The moment you release control of someone's salvation, you are free to simply love them unconditionally as God does.

Does this mean we should never have conversations with people who are deconstructing, hoping to persuade them to the truth of the gospel of Jesus? Of course not. The point is that it's imperative for us to surrender their salvation to the Lord while being emotionally and relationally aware. In that moment, the priest was able to be a non-anxious presence in the face of a crisis of faith. He didn't see himself as Augustine's savior, needing to intervene to save him from his heresy. His advice to Monica? "Just pray to God for him." He knew that only God could intervene in Augustine's life.

STRESS TEST

As you walk with someone who is deconstructing, you quickly realize that deconstruction is not just a crisis of faith for them; it's a stress test for *your* faith too. It challenges you to lean on the beliefs you confess. Do you believe that God saves? Do you believe that God is sovereign? Do you believe that God can handle hard questions? Do you believe that God can handle intense emotions? Do you believe that this whole thing is true, even when it's held up against critical scrutiny?

When someone is deconstructing, they might bring questions, problems, critiques, and ideas that you find intimidating. Maybe you've never thought of them before. Maybe you've had the same questions, but they never bothered you the way they're bothering them. There are lots of things you might be hearing for the first time. It's not unlikely that you'll feel in over your head.

That's okay. You don't need to have all the answers. The truth is that no one has all the answers. I hope someone else's deconstruction pushes you to grow in your faith. But your presence in their life is so much more important than your ability to answer every question. Your demeanor matters more than your apologetics. If we enter these relationships with all of the answers but full of fear, anxiety, and control, it doesn't matter how good our apologetics are. You can't change someone's mind if their heart hasn't been won.

We can't stop people from having a crisis of faith, but what we can do is foster environments—including the "environment" of individual relationships—that create enough sense of belonging and safety that the intensity of the crisis isn't nearly as high as it has the potential to be.

So the question for us becomes, How can we be a non-anxious presence in their life to help them break free of imaginative gridlock, become unstuck, and be able to imagine other ways of faithfully following Jesus that are free from the shackles of a performative, fundamentalist faith?

A NON-ANXIOUS PRESENCE

When someone is deconstructing their faith, relationships become sensitive in ways that they may not have been before. So how can you be a non-anxious presence and help this person process their deconstruction in a way that renews their faith rather than destroying it? You are not going to do this perfectly. It takes discernment, wisdom, and high levels of trust to understand what a person needs at any moment. There's no way to prescribe a one-size-fits-all approach for how to handle these relationships.

This section is not designed to be a tool used to "work on" the person who is deconstructing as a "project." The six postures I will suggest in this section are not meant as silver bullets to "fix" your friend, family member, or congregant of their doubts and questions and pull them out of their deconstruction. The goal of these postures is no less than *love*. These postures are meant to help you express God's love and your love for them in a way that will be received while they are processing the difficulties of their deconstruction.

The six postures are prayer, patience, persistence, calm, curiosity, and care. The goal is to be a faithful presence in their life so that they see the beauty of Christ through you. They are out of your control and in God's hands. All you can do is assume these postures and wait on the Lord.

Prayer. By lifting someone up in prayer, we are releasing our control of them and actively trusting them to the Lord's good providence. Prayer is the surest way to say to God, "Not my will, but yours be done."

In prayer, we bring our fears, worries, and anxieties about our loved ones to the Lord and ask him to do what only he can do. We acknowledge our weakness and dependence on him. We ask for forgiveness for feeling impatient and angry. We ask for his mercy in our lives as we release control, and in their life as they search for the life that is only found in Christ.

In our conversations with them, it's tempting to lean on our own wisdom and persuasiveness, our emotional appeals and clever logic to try and "win them back for Christ." Prayer forces us to recognize that we have no power to save another image bearer. Prayer fixes our eyes on Christ and takes them off our own illusory ability to save someone.

It also takes the pressure off us. When we are no longer in charge of saving someone, we are free to love them instead of fixing them. What matters more is our character, our devotion to the Lord, and our simple testifying to the goodness of the gospel of Christ, rather than our ability to persuade and argue. There are no results for you to show God at heaven's gates. God hasn't given every individual a salvation quota. What he has called you to do is to follow him, become like him, and let your light shine before others.

Patience. With releasing control to God in prayer comes patience. We shouldn't expect someone to "reconstruct" their faith overnight, or in a month, or even in a year. The revivalist expectations of American evangelicalism have led us to think that true transformation happens in a moment. Sometimes it does, but most of the time it doesn't. We need to allow others time to work through their doubts, questions, concerns, and wanderings and give the Lord time to work in *his* way, not ours.

The apostle Paul is a fascinating case study in this. We often focus on Paul's dramatic conversion on the road to Damascus. This seems to play into our light-switch way of thinking about salvation. We forget that, as he recounts his conversion in Galatians 1, he says after his conversion, he didn't go speak with even the other apostles. He went away to the Arabian desert for three years just to process the new revelation he had encountered. How much more time do we need to process our thoughts, beliefs, and feelings about Jesus, the church, and everything that comes with them? How much more time do we need to think through the implications of a Risen King?

We need to develop holy patience as the practice of releasing our control to God. Patience honors their need to work through their beliefs. We must see a longer horizon of time than the moment right in front of us. Change doesn't happen overnight, and we can't make anyone change. We must be patient people waiting on a patient God who has mercy on those who doubt.

Persistence. When someone is deconstructing their faith, you might find them drifting away from the relationship. That's most likely not because they don't want to have a relationship with you, but because they don't know where they fit in the relationship anymore. If they *don't* want a relationship anymore, I'd ask them why. It might be for some other reason besides their changing beliefs, in which case, it might be best to work on repairing the relationship and let someone else discuss the spiritual side of things with them. In fact, mending that wound might be the biggest testimony you can give them.

But if they do want a relationship and aren't sure how to move forward, continue to invite them over to your house for meals, hang out, let your kids play together, and go to events in the community with them. People cannot heal in isolation; they heal in community with others. Be persistent in your relationship with them.

You don't have to be pesky to be persistent. If they have decided to put up some boundaries around the relationship, it's important to honor those. Persistence isn't about being annoying, overbearing, or trying to shove a gospel presentation into every conversation. It's about maintaining the relationship to the best of your ability. To continue to provide a place for them to belong and feel safe in your presence. Be persistent in your love for them the way the Lord is persistent in his love for you.

Calm. When someone is deconstructing their faith, everything feels like it's on the line. It's understandable that you will feel worried about it. Your heart rate starts to rise, your palms begin to sweat, you get a lump in your throat, and you start to fear for their salvation. You might get angry, wondering how they could do this, mad that they would do something that could threaten your relationship. All of these are normal and valid emotions, but we must not let our emotions get the best of us.

Remember what they are experiencing, the courage it took to talk with you, and how difficult the process of deconstruction is. Thank them for trusting you enough to share with you. Affirm their experience where you feel like you can. Let them know that you are a safe person to talk to.

It does no good to try and control someone through your emotions. They must be moving toward you, which means that you must be a safe person for them to move toward.[4] This means regulating your emotions and managing your reactions. "Blessed are the peacemakers," Jesus told his disciples. Making peace in the relationship by demonstrating self-control over your own reactions can be the difference between building trust and a lost relationship.

Curiosity. A friend of mine told me that when he first told his dad that he had questions about Christianity, his dad immediately asked him, "Well, do you know where you're going to go when you die?" My friend told me, at that moment, he knew he couldn't talk to his dad about any of these things. Because his dad just didn't get it. He was focused on one thing: Are you going to heaven when you die? He didn't truly *see* my friend with the questions, the concerns, and the grief that he felt in his crisis. He didn't need his dad to try to save him. He needed his dad's love for him no matter where this journey led him. Not that he just wanted to know where he was going to go when he died or that he had all the right answers on his doctrinal test.

Fourteen percent of people who dechurched cited that a parent's inability to listen contributed to their dechurching.[5] What would have happened if, instead of going straight to questioning his salvation, my friend's dad had been curious about what he was going through? What if he had said things like, "Tell me about the process that got you here," "What have been some concerns you have that maybe I missed?" "What has been the hardest part of all of this for you?" "Now that you're here, what is the scariest thing for you now?" or even "Tell me about the last time you really felt that God loved you." I can imagine the conversation would have looked drastically different.

Curiosity has been called the "secret juice of relationships."[6] It lowers people's guard. They expected you to be upset, but instead, you were curious. Instead of reacting, you engaged. Instead of shrugging them off, you took an interest in them. Being curious about their doubts, struggles, and concerns is one of the most powerful things you can do. You might learn more than you think.

By being curious and asking questions, you can get to a layer beneath the doubt, to the thing that catalyzed the doubt in the first place. That's where you want to be. Addressing doubt is like addressing a symptom without ever looking at the cause. It's only by remaining calm and being curious that you will ever get to the root cause of the doubt. And it's there at the root that you will find their heart.

Care. The biggest temptation you will face when walking with someone who is deconstructing is to see them as a project to undertake, a problem to be fixed. When all you see is a problem instead of a person, it's impossible to truly care for them. You're so focused on trying to set them straight that you miss the pain of the person sitting in front of you. We must switch from a "fixing" mentality that is born out of fear to a caring mentality that is born out of love.

Just as we are wounded from broken relationships, so too are wounds healed through relationships. When someone's trust has been broken in the church, God, or other Christians, that trust can only be healed through a relationship with someone else. That someone, I hope, is you. But that means bearing with them in patience, carrying their burden when it feels too heavy for them to carry alone, and having faith for them when they don't have faith for themselves.

In *The Fellowship of the Ring*, when Frodo is given the Ring of Power and is about to set off on his journey to destroy the ring alone, his friends Merry, Pippin, and Sam all insist that they go on the journey with him. After many attempts to convince them to let him go alone, Frodo finally admits, "But it does not seem that I can trust anyone." To which Merry replies, "It all depends on what you want. You can trust us to stick to you through thick and thin—to the bitter end. And you can trust us to keep any secret of yours—closer than you keep it to yourself. But you cannot trust us to let you face trouble alone, and go off without a word. We are your friends, Frodo."[7]

This is the type of care someone who is deconstructing needs. Someone who can keep their trust, stick with them through thick and thin, allow them to share their secrets and keep them safe, and who will not let them face trouble alone and go off without a word. You act as the hand that holds them even as they might wander away from the flock.

REMAINING FAITHFUL IN THE STRESS TEST

As we talk about these postures that we should take when walking with someone who is deconstructing, it's important for us and for them that we resolve to stay faithful in our own life and doctrine (1 Timothy 4:16). When we're facing the stress test of someone else's deconstruction, it can be far too easy to buckle under its weight in the name of love.

For just one example, it's common for someone to profess a historic view of the Christian sexual ethic until a child, friend, or congregant comes out to them. While that should fill us with compassion, it shouldn't shatter our faith. Sometimes it feels like the loving thing to do is to capitulate, or even just waffle a little, in a conflict to try and make someone feel loved and accepted. However, when you waver in your convictions, it validates their doubts about whether there is anything real about the faith or not. If it was that easy to change your mind, did you ever believe it to begin with? In the context of the other postures, it's good to lovingly, graciously, and kindly stand your ground.

That doesn't mean we should be closed-minded. Curiosity, compassion, and conviction doesn't have to be a "pick two" dilemma. We must be rooted in God, anchored with a hope that can't be shaken. We can trust that even if we don't have the answer or the solution to someone's questions, God does.

Augustine tells another story of a time when his belief in Manichaeism was waning, but he still wasn't convinced of Christianity. He told his mother this, and, after years of tearful prayers, she wasn't as excited at the news the way he expected her to be. He writes, "Her anxiety had already been allayed. For in her prayers to you she wept for me as though I were dead, but she also knew that you would recall me to life."[8] He goes on to say about Monica, "She had no doubt that I must pass through this condition, which would lead me from sickness to health, but not before I had surmounted a still graver danger, much like that which doctors call the crisis."[9] Monica had become a non-anxious presence. She knew there was no way she could save her son. She had surrendered control to God in prayer and knew Augustine's only way out of his crisis of faith was through it.

When all of this is put together, it should look like what Davis and Graham call quiet, calm, curiosity. They write, "The simplest way it should look is quiet, calm, curiosity. When we are strong in our knowledge of God and our experience of him, our firm foundation should give us a calm and curious demeanor concerning others. Our goal is not to argue people into the kingdom of God. Certainly we can give well-reasoned explanations for our faith, but the key distinction is that we do so by persuading them with a better story."[10]

This posture is a far cry from the loud denouncements of woke agendas, cancel culture, and demonic Democrats. Is it okay to have your concerns? Of course. But our character in how we approach and articulate our convictions and concerns with love and grace is just as important as our ability to stand on our convictions with faithful resolve.

Paul wrote in Colossians, "Let your speech always be gracious, seasoned with salt, so that you may know how you should answer each person" (Colossians 4:6). This isn't about letting falsehood go unchallenged. It's about knowing how you should answer someone in gracious ways that bring out the flavor of God's love, remembering that it is God's kindness that leads us to repentance (Romans 2:4), and it is not on us to bring God's judgment down on our friend, child, or sibling, but to represent God by modeling his love to them. We are Christ's ambassadors; he is making his appeal to them through us (2 Corinthians 5:20). May we represent our crucified king with the same humility, grace, and patience that he loved us with.

RECONSTRUCTING
SUFFERING

THOSE WHO ARE DECONSTRUCTING are experiencing a crisis: the loss of God. That crisis was brought about because their faith couldn't hold the weight of their compounded anxieties. One of the reasons that their faith couldn't hold under pressure is because of the up-and-to-the-right spirituality they were handed in evangelicalism. Going through periods of spiritual drought in a trough is a natural part of the life of faith, but for many, they were never shown how trials, loss, and suffering are ways that our faith is built. With the foundation of faith cracked and the walls of the house rotted, it's easy to see how even the smallest flame—not to mention volcanic infernos—might set a house of faith ablaze. Everyone has anxieties that accumulate over time through the hardships of life in a variety of ways. I'm not talking specifically about clinical anxiety—though that certainly counts—but all the things we encounter that make it difficult to live an integrated life. Each anxiety might be big or small, but they compound over time until we collapse under their weight.

Some of these anxieties might include things like death, abuse, adultery, gossip, racism, infertility, betrayal, injustice, divorce, sexuality, hypocrisy, mental health, misinformation, politics, division, and conspiracy theories. Each one of those could be double-clicked and reveal a hundred variations. What we need is a theology of suffering to help those who suffer see God at work in the darkest parts of their lives.

In my own story, I can point back to the adverse childhood experiences that compounded into the anxiety I was unable to bear. My parents' abuse and addiction; being taken from my parents at a young age; losing my grandmother, other family members, and mother to death; my mentor abusing my friends; the doubts and questions that I had about the Bible, my church, and my faith—each of these was a major anxiety. That's not to mention all of the small anxieties I had accumulated along the way, such as my frequent conflicts in Bible class and a general sense of not fitting in with the Christian culture I was in.

As Alan Noble writes in *On Getting Out of Bed*, "Despite the comforts of contemporary life and its promises of even greater peace and self-mastery, life is terribly hard. A comfortable, pleasant life isn't normal. . . . It is undeniably true that day-to-day life demands a great deal of courage."[1] The courage to face the difficulties of life doesn't come from the removal of sufferings, but from trusting in the Lord and seeking refuge in him. Doing that requires us to believe that God is good in our suffering, not despising or abandoning us, but forming us, giving us hope, and filling us with love. Being Christlike involves suffering, because Christ himself suffered on our behalf. And one of the primary ways God makes us more Christlike—if we have the eyes to see and the will to submit—is through suffering.

MARY'S DOUBT

The siblings Mary, Martha, and Lazarus were dear friends of Jesus. Once, when Jesus had been warmly welcomed into their home, Martha busied herself with preparations in the kitchen while Mary sat at Jesus' feet, absorbing his teachings. Martha had accused Mary of not helping her with all the things that needed to be done, but

Jesus had said to Martha, "Mary has made the right choice, and it will not be taken away from her" (Luke 10:42).

Time passed. Now Lazarus was sick, and his illness was getting worse. The sisters sent word to Jesus: "The one you love is sick." But Jesus delayed. By the time he approached, Lazarus had died. Martha, heartbroken yet hopeful, spoke to Jesus, "Lord, if you had been here, my brother wouldn't have died. Yet even now I know that whatever you ask from God, God will give you" (John 11:21-22). Mary, who before had sat at Jesus' feet, now kept her distance, staying in the house instead of going to meet him with her sister.

When Jesus and Mary finally met, Mary's anguish mirrored Martha's, but without Martha's faith. Mary fell at Jesus' feet in sorrow and said, "Lord, if you had been here, my brother wouldn't have died!" refraining from the hope of Jesus' power to resurrect Lazarus, which Martha had displayed. Jesus, deeply moved, asked, "Where have you put him?" Then, in shared sorrow for the loss of a brother and friend, Jesus wept.

It was only after this public display of grief that Jesus performed the unimaginable: raising Lazarus from the dead. There was no miracle without heartache, no joy without pain. Before Jesus performed his final miracle, he disappointed Mary, one of his closest and most beloved disciples and friends. The faith of one of his most faithful followers was tested through Jesus' absence in a time of need. How could he do this? Why would he let Mary down by not saving Lazarus from death when it was in his power to do so? What kind of God would allow us to suffer?

A FRAMEWORK FOR SUFFERING

Earlier in the book, we discussed how American evangelicalism's understanding of God's role in our suffering is lacking. We're ill-prepared for suffering, swayed by a diluted gospel that promises ease. We often wonder, "Why do bad things happen to good people?" rather than, "How do these events shape us into Christ's image?"

Jesus spoke of those who embrace the word with joy but falter during hardships (Matthew 13:20-21). How can we fortify our hearts against such faltering? Suffering must be integral to our picture of discipleship. Alongside learning Scripture and doctrine, Christians should be prepared for trials. As a teacher of mine once said, "We do theology in the light so we can stand on it in the dark."[2] Preparing for suffering doesn't diminish its pain, but it might bolster our faith in the middle of it. How should we approach this?

Most of our efforts in discipleship focus on the high-control elements in our life, like listening to good Bible teaching and getting into community, as well as personal practices such as Bible reading and prayer. These are good, and we should emphasize them. But we also need to emphasize the low-control elements of spiritual formation, namely suffering.[3]

Romans 5:3-5 provides us with a framework for understanding suffering's redemptive role in the Christian life. Paul says, "Not only so, but we also glory in our sufferings, because we know that suffering produces perseverance; perseverance, character; and character, hope. And hope does not put us to shame" (NIV). Apparently for Paul, suffering isn't something to be avoided; in fact, he finds suffering something to be *gloried in*. How do we find glory in our suffering? Through the cycle he describes: suffering, perseverance, character, and hope.

Suffering. Everything in our culture tells us to avoid suffering at all costs. Suffering, we're told, is an enemy to our flourishing. You see this explicitly in deconstruction and exvangelical circles. *The Liturgists* podcast show description reads, "The Liturgists are committed to helping humanity love more and suffer less by bravely exploring our unique individuality within community and without judgment."[4] It's enticing, isn't it? On the surface, who wouldn't want to love more and suffer less?

Escaping suffering is presented as a key part of fulfilling your potential, finding healing, and living a life of purpose, meaning, and health. Elisabeth Elliot, the famous missionary to the Auca people in Ecuador—the people who famously murdered her husband, Jim Elliot—defines suffering simply as "Having what you don't want or wanting what you don't have."[5] As she says, that covers pretty much everything. A death in the family, a cancer diagnosis, infertility, sexual abuse, singleness, betrayal of trust, abuse of power, wrestling with sexuality, divorce, doubts about God, depression, anxiety, poverty, injustice, racism. All of these are examples of having what you don't want or wanting what you don't have. These are the anxieties that accumulate throughout our lives and wear down our faith.

Not all suffering is equal—some people experience the horrors of sin and evil in ways we couldn't imagine—but in most cases, it does no good to compare sufferings. We all suffer in our own ways. When we suffer, we don't need someone telling us that other people have it worse. We need to know that there is hope in the midst of pain, light on the other side of darkness, that our suffering has meaning, and that it isn't for nothing.

But wishing to never suffer is like wishing the moon wouldn't circle the earth. We will all experience suffering on this side of eternity. The risk of love is never divorced from the risk of suffering. We can try to avoid all the darkness of the world, but we would never see the light of love. The Lord didn't promise deliverance from the valley of the shadow of death; he promised to accompany us in it.

There is a way to allow suffering to do its work in us and shape us into the image of Christ. It starts when we begin *embracing* our suffering. We don't have to wish suffering on ourselves, but we do need to make our peace with it. Having lost nearly everyone in my family and experienced multiple significant wounds by churches, I can attest that there comes a point when you begin to become familiar with suffering. The pain of suffering isn't reduced in any way, but you begin to remember the same feelings as you experience them over and over again. Eventually, you realize that no matter what you suffer, it doesn't have to break you.

As David says in Psalm 27,

The LORD is my light and my salvation—
whom should I fear?
The LORD is the stronghold of my life—
whom should I dread? (Psalm 27:1)

Suffering, counterintuitively, is a means of grace in our lives. It releases the illusion of control we have over our lives. It brings our weakness into the light and reveals our need for help from a power greater than ourselves. Instead of trying to escape suffering, the Christian looks at suffering and sees Christ on the cross, hanging there in our place. The Christian knows that to be united with Christ is to be "crucified with Christ" (Galatians 2:20) and to "share in his sufferings in order that we may also share in his glory" (Romans 8:17 NIV).

In *The Second Mountain*, David Brooks writes, "The right thing to do in moments of suffering is to stand erect in the suffering. Wait. See what it has to teach you. Understand that your suffering is a task that, if handled correctly, with the help of others, will lead to enlargement, not diminishment."[6]

There are two ways suffering can change you. The first is by breaking you down, leaving you afraid, paranoid, and void of hope. The other is by breaking you open, leaving you with a wider heart, and expanding your capacity for love. Jesus, in his suffering, was broken open for us. When we share in Christ's sufferings, we too are broken open and able to love others more than we could before.

Because of the suffering you have endured in the past, you are able to persevere and endure even more suffering in the future. Each season of suffering prepares you for the next one. As you persevere in suffering, you become more resilient in the face of trials.

Perseverance. Every runner will tell you that the first mile is a lie. As you start, your body protests. You start to think that you can't keep going. This discomfort makes many, including me, consider stopping.

But it's a lie. Beyond this initial wall is the "runner's high," typically around the second or third mile. The discomfort doesn't vanish but morphs into almost a euphoric sensation due to endorphins released when you push past your perceived limits. If you halt at the initial discomfort, running is just pain. But if you push through to the runner's high, running is more than pain. It's joy.

The same principle at work in the runner's high is present in suffering, except the result isn't a high produced by endorphins. It's the love of God poured out in our hearts produced by the character and hope we develop through perseverance. But we can only persevere by accepting our suffering and finding joy in it. Yes, *joy*.

Hearing that we should find joy in our suffering is offensive to our modern ears. Yet that's exactly what James, Jesus' brother, admonishes us to do: "Consider it pure joy, my brothers and sisters, whenever you face trials of many kinds, because you know that the testing of your faith produces perseverance" (James 1:2-3 NIV). There are those words *joy*, *trials*, and *perseverance* again. These three are inextricably intertwined. The Christian posture toward suffering isn't avoidance but perseverance and joy.

The writer of Hebrews said of Jesus, "For the joy set before him he endured the cross, scorning its shame, and sat down at the right hand of the throne of God" (Hebrews 12:2 NIV). Jesus endured the cross; he persevered through its pain and shame for the joy on the other side when he rose from the dead, sat on his throne, defeated Satan, sin, and death, and brought salvation to his people.

How did Jesus endure the cross? By following the example he set for his disciples when he gave them the Lord's Prayer. "Your kingdom come. Your will be done on earth as it is in heaven" (Matthew 6:10). The night before his crucifixion, we see Jesus sweating blood, having a panic attack moments before his arrest, surrendering his desire to avoid suffering to his Father. "My Father, if it is possible, let this cup pass from me. Yet not as I will, but as you will" (Matthew 26:39). Jesus trusts his Father more than his desire to escape pain. He knows the

Father has a purpose in the suffering and will accomplish his will through it. By enduring the suffering, God's kingdom will be more manifest on earth than it was before. Ultimately, Jesus trusts the Father and submits to the suffering before him.

In submitting to suffering, Jesus absorbs and transforms it into our salvation. Hanging on the cross, the sky went black, and Jesus absorbed the darkness of the world into his body and spirit. Overtaken by it, he lay in the grave for three days. On Easter morning, he was raised in victory over death, defeating the darkness that overtook him on the cross with the light of life.

This is what it means to persevere. While suffering is the result of the evil and brokenness of the world, we, like Christ, absorb the darkness of suffering into our bodies, transform it, and release it back into the world as light. We absorb hate and release it back into the world as love. We absorb lies and release them back into the world as truth. We absorb death and release it back into the world as life. We don't see ourselves as simply victims of suffering but as agents of transformation who mock death and scorn shame, knowing that God's victorious rule and reign over all evil will be made manifest through our perseverance.[7]

It's important to distinguish between enduring suffering and enabling abuse. While all suffering stems from the effects of sin in the world, some sufferings arise from abuse, oppression, and injustice. Consider abusive marriages, child abuse, or systemic injustices like Jim Crow laws and abortion. Enduring suffering doesn't mean tolerating abuse. Victims should seek escape, children need protection, and unjust systems require change. Enduring isn't enabling. No one should remain in abuse under the guise of "faithful endurance." Abusive systems and relationships must be dismantled; any contrary advice misrepresents Jesus' teachings.

It's possible to escape abuse and still persevere in suffering. Because enduring suffering is about transforming the pain we experience and releasing it back into the world for the sake of others, just as Jesus did for us. For Jesus, the cross was both suffering and joy. And he endured it *for us*. As Augustine wrote in his *Confessions,* "It is not as though I do not suffer wounds, but I feel rather that you heal them over and over again."[8]

Character. Anyone who has lost a loved one will tell you that you never truly heal from it. The pain might lessen in its acuteness over time, but it never goes away. The sting of loss can be triggered at any time, seemingly out of nowhere. Our deepest wounds don't disappear; they scar over. You don't simply heal from suffering; you are changed by it.

Like scars that leave marks on our bodies that will never fade away, suffering irreversibly marks our souls. When the Covid-19 pandemic began, we were originally told to stay inside for two weeks to "flatten the curve," and then we would all return to our normal lives. How naive we were to think that we were ever returning to the way things were in 2019! There was no going back, only going through.

The lockdowns reshaped us—for better or for worse. Many entered the pandemic with friends who abandoned them in the midst of the chaos. Family and friends were lost in rabbit holes of conspiracy theories and political polarization. People were looking for a way to relieve their suffering by finding quick fixes and easy answers. If they could just find the source of the virus, blame the right people, or protest the right thing, then everything would get better. They didn't absorb and transform the darkness of the world; they were overtaken by it and transformed into its image.

But there is another way. Persevering through suffering the way Jesus did, submitting to God's will to use it, absorbing, transforming it, and releasing it back into the world as light, life, and love forms our character. Suffering opens windows in our souls to see things previously hidden from us in ways that nothing else can.

Suffering shows us our inability to control the path of our life. We plan our life as if nothing will change. We assume that our loved one will be here tomorrow, that our bank account and pantry will be full, that our body will stay healthy, that the people we trust are actually trustworthy, and a thousand other things we take for granted. Suffering rushes into our presumption of safety like a wrecking ball, revealing the frailty of our frame.

When this happens, there are only a few ways to respond. The first is by swearing it will never happen again. You erect protective barriers around yourself to keep away all potential harm. You withdraw from any environment or relationship that even resembles what caused the pain before. You avoid taking risks, close yourself off from others, and refuse to be found vulnerable. You grasp what little you have left, refusing to open your hands, fearing that what you have might also be taken away from you.

The other way is by surrendering it to the loving care of the Lord. Instead of closing your hands around what you have, you open your hands to what God might have for you. You "humble [yourself], therefore, under the mighty hand of God, so that he may exalt you at the proper time, casting all your cares on him, because he cares about you" (1 Peter 5:6-7).

Instead of closing yourself off from vulnerability, you give your vulnerability to others as a gift. Instead of turning inward and looking at yourself, you look outward and see others. You see their pain, heartbreak, and suffering, and your heart grows larger, making more space for them. Paul demonstrated this to the church in Corinth when he said,

> As God's ministers, we commend ourselves in everything: by great endurance, by afflictions, by hardships, by difficulties, by beatings, by imprisonments, by riots, by labors, by sleepless nights, by times of hunger, by purity, by knowledge, by patience, by kindness, by the Holy Spirit, by sincere love, by the word of truth, by the power of God; through weapons of righteousness for the right hand and the left, through glory and dishonor, through slander and good report; regarded as deceivers, yet true;

as unknown, yet recognized; as dying, yet see—we live; as being disciplined, yet not killed; as grieving, yet always rejoicing; as poor, yet enriching many; as having nothing, yet possessing everything. We have spoken openly to you, Corinthians; our heart has been opened wide. We are not withholding our affection from you. (2 Corinthians 6:4-12)

Through all of Paul's hardships, he said, "Our heart has been opened wide. We are not withholding our affection from you." Paul allowed the suffering of his ministry to open his heart wide for others. Through enduring, he learned knowledge, patience, kindness, sincere love, the word of truth, the power of God, discipline, rejoicing, enriching many, contentedness, and more. Paul was shaped by his pain. Likewise, our suffering shapes us when we open our hands to God and our hearts to others.

Hope. As suffering forms our character into the character of Christ, it doesn't terminate on ourselves but points us to Christ himself. As we grow closer to the king, we long for the king's rule and reign in our hearts and over the whole world. We groan with creation, waiting for his return to redeem the brokenness of this world. In this way, our character becomes more than virtues we embody; it becomes hope itself. Hope that the king will return to do what he promised to do: make all things new.

At the end of John's revelation, he sees the new Jerusalem, God's dwelling place, coming from the clouds to be joined again to earth. After he sees the glorious city, John says,

Then I heard a loud voice from the throne: Look, God's dwelling is with humanity, and he will live with them. They will be his peoples, and God himself will be with them and will be their God. He will wipe away every tear from their eyes. Death will be no more; grief, crying, and pain will be no more, because the previous things have passed away. (Revelation 21:3-4)

As we absorb the pain of the world in our bodies to be transformed, we long for the day when there will be no more pain at all; when the all-pervasive love of God will transform the whole world. We wait for what Habakkuk prophesied, that "the earth will be filled with the knowledge of the LORD's glory, as the water covers the sea" (Habakkuk 2:14).

Hope is a necessary ingredient for enduring and transforming suffering. Otherwise, there is nothing past the pain. There is no guarantee that the wrongs of the world will be made right. Without hope to pull our eyes up and to the Lord, our eyes are hopelessly stuck on ourselves. We can't see the light of the future, only the darkness of the present.

Tim Keller writes, "Human beings are hope-shaped creatures. The way you live now is completely controlled by what you believe about your future." He continues:

> Do you believe that when you die, you rot? That life in this world is all the happiness you will ever get? Do you believe that someday the sun is going to die and all human civilization is going to be gone, and nobody will remember anything anyone has ever done? That's one way to imagine your future. But here's another. Do you believe in 'new heavens and new earth'? Do you believe in a Judgment Day when every evil deed and injustice will be redressed? Do you believe you are headed for a future of endless joy? Those are two utterly different futures, and depending on which one you believe, you are going to handle your dungeons, your suffering, in two utterly different ways.[9]

Without the hope of the king and his kingdom, we're left with only ourselves and our sorrows. We're abandoned to Sheol, lost in the domain of darkness. But when we lift our eyes to the one who our help comes from, we see a kingdom that can't be shaken, gates that even hell can't prevail against. Our hope in him carries us through the darkest night of the soul. Even when we can't see what is ahead of us, we rest on his promise that one day we will see in full what we now only see in part.

We are shaped by what we hope for. If we hope in the Lord, the horizon of our hope is as high as the heavens, as deep as the sea, and as wide as the east is from the west. This hope doesn't disappoint us because we have the testimony of God's faithfulness to his people in Scripture, the saints throughout history, and our own lives. Because of that, we can trust that he will be faithful to his promise to make everything sad untrue and all things new.

This is the gift of suffering: to become people of love who are held in the love of God and extend God's love to others. Suffering is a crucible of formation, an instrument in God's hands to fashion us into his image. Only in this light can we say that what was meant for evil against us, God used for our good. Because of this we can truly say, "It is well, it is well with my soul."

MARY'S HOPE

Soon after Jesus raised Lazarus, he returned to Bethany, where Lazarus, Mary, and Martha were for Passover. The four of them invited others over for dinner, and, while they were eating, Mary took out her jar of perfume, anointed Jesus' feet, and wiped his feet with her hair. Immediately, people at the party started to question her. The perfume was expensive, worth a whole year's wages. Why would she waste it by pouring it on Jesus' feet?

The same Mary who not long ago stayed inside, keeping her distance from Jesus, angry and full of doubt by his delay in her time of need, now emptied her most expensive possession on his feet. Now, she found Jesus more valuable than her most valuable belonging. She once doubted him, but now he was worth everything to her.

When the other guests questioned her for this seemingly irresponsible act, John records, "Jesus answered, 'Leave her alone; she has kept it for the day of my burial'" (John 12:7). Mary didn't know it, but Jesus knew that this was an anointing for his death. Jesus brought Mary's brother back from the grave, but he was about to enter his own grave. He would suffer once and for all so that death would be defeated and God's restoration project would begin. Mary's sorrow became her character, and her character produced hope that Jesus would indeed, one day soon, be king over everything.

10

RECONSTRUCTING BELIEF

Harry Potter, an orphan with a lightning-shaped scar, was raised under the "care" of his Aunt Petunia and Uncle Vernon. They kept him in the dark about his magical family, relegating him to a cupboard under the stairs and feeding him lies about his parents' death.

Despite the mundane life at Number Four Privet Drive, peculiar events—such as his hair inexplicably regrowing immediately after a haircut, and a conversation with a boa constrictor—hinted at the truth that was hidden from Harry. The turning point came with Rubeus Hagrid's revelation: "You're a wizard, Harry." Suddenly, Harry was thrust into his identity as The Boy Who Lived, destined for Hogwarts and the eventual battle with the Dark Lord Voldemort, the wizard who murdered his parents.

Harry didn't know who he was because the story he'd been told was a lie. Even when he saw strange things around him that called everything he thought he knew into question, he had no way of making sense of them because he didn't know the true story. He was living a lie; a lie that was told to him from an early age. If it hadn't been for Hagrid delivering him a letter from a world beyond his imagination, he would have believed the wrong story forever and never have known who he truly was.

While deconstruction is primarily a crisis of faith, that crisis is worked out in a day-to-day struggle at the level of our beliefs. It's easy to think that your beliefs are primarily a cognitive function, a matter of what you intellectually assent to and what you reject as false. But as we've seen earlier in this book, our beliefs are much more complex than that. What you believe isn't the product of mere intellectual pursuit; it's the result of the world you imagine to be real. And that imagination isn't formed simply by axiomatic statements of truth, but by the stories you believe, consciously and unconsciously. The story you believe to be true about God, the world, and yourself will have much more to do with your beliefs than a statement of faith.

Cultural Christianity tells us the wrong story about reality. It gridlocks our imagination through either the legalism or licentiousness that is produced by moralistic therapeutic deism. That's why reconstruction isn't just a matter of affirming the right doctrines as true, but a matter of *inhabiting an entirely different story*. It's committing to and orienting your life around an existential map that directs your whole self—heart, soul, mind, strength, and relationships—toward God.[1] And to do that, you need to understand the false stories that we believe and the true story that God is writing and has invited us into.

THE FALSE STORIES WE BELIEVE

What's true for Harry Potter is true for us. We have all believed false stories. In Romans, Paul says that we have exchanged the truth for a lie and have worshiped what is created instead of the Creator himself (Romans 1:25). All sin is the result of believing a lie instead of the truth and misplacing our worship. The Bible calls this idolatry.

Underneath all our sins is idolatry. Idolatry is not something that we end up doing by accident but is our default mode of being. The idols of this world are not sitting on a bench waiting to be chosen; they are forcing themselves on us, demanding our worship by feeding us lies that sound like the truth. They take the power that God originally gave to humans, and they use it against us.[2] Idols capture our hearts by telling us lies and sweeping us into false stories. When these false stories come into conflict with the revelation of God's true story, there is a profound disorientation that happens. The story that God tells and the stories that idols tell can't both be true. One of them must give.

But the lies we believe have seemed like the truth for so long. The truthfulness of God's story isn't always obvious. When the stories the idols tell us are baked into our society, the lies that snatch away God's worship are strengthened by social structural supports. We are whispered lies by the idols of this world, lies that our fallen natures *want* to believe, and our society says are normal, maybe even celebrated.[3]

Some of these false stories might be things like individualism (I am my own and belong to myself), romanticism (the only truth is what feels right), nationalism (my nation is special to God), progressivism (the world is progressing on its own, I only have to hop on board), or empiricism (the only truth is what I can prove to be true). These stories shape our imaginations and habituate us into a reality that is contrary to God's story. What is even scarier is that these stories can twist parts of God's story and incorporate them into their own story to make Christianity a means to their own ends. When Christianity is a means to the ends of some other story, we have lost the plot entirely.

This isn't to say that someone who is deconstructing is somehow more susceptible to believing false stories. We are *all* captured by lies in one way or another. We shouldn't look down on them as particularly weak and ourselves as strong. It's worth examining our own lives to see where we are worshiping an idol instead of God.

The need, then, is for us to keep ourselves positioned in God's story: the grand narrative of creation, fall, redemption, and restoration. If the biblical story does not control our thinking, then we will be swept into the story that the world tells about itself.[4]

DOCTRINE AS STORY

How do we keep ourselves in that story? Surprisingly, this is where doctrine comes in. Doctrine has often been seen as a Scantron test to get into heaven when you die. If you pass, you're in. If you fail, it's eternal damnation for you. And while it is important to affirm truth and deny lies, the role doctrine plays in the life of a Christian is much more than a simple answer to a test. When doctrine is put in its proper place, it reveals to us the script of God's story and the role that we play in it.[5]

If you think about your favorite movie franchise, whether that's Marvel, Harry Potter, Lord of the Rings, Star Wars, or any other, there are common elements in the movies that let you know which cinematic universe you are in. Marvel has superheroes. Harry Potter has Hogwarts, hippogriffs, and wands. Lord of the Rings has hobbits, elves, and magic rings. Star Wars has lightsabers, spaceships, the Jedi, and the Sith. The Force, the Ring of Power, and *expecto patronum* are all magic, but they are different kinds of magic. All of these elements tip you off to which story you are in. Each story has different laws that govern it.

For Christians, doctrine functions in the same way as the elements of the various cinematic universes. Doctrine helps Christians know they are living in the right story. God as Trinity; Jesus as both fully God and fully man; humanity as divine image-bearing but sinful creatures living in a broken world; Jesus living a perfect life, dying, and rising again to defeat death and forgive our sins; and the promise that one day Jesus will return as king over all creation to make all things new. These doctrines don't just serve as answers to a test but as the script of a story.[6]

Doctrine is a description of reality. And when doctrine functions more like a script than a test, it's freeing rather than restrictive. It allows you to see the world the way that it *actually* is because you're looking at it through the right lens, you're reading the right script. You're quite literally *living in reality*.

This doesn't answer every question we have, but it does put many fears and anxieties at ease. We're not writing our own story and wondering why things don't happen according to it. We're not deceived by the stories of this world that try to commoditize our humanity. We can wield the truth to see through lies and rightly direct our worship to God alone. Our feeling of peace is directly correlated with the direction of our worship. When we worship God alone in Spirit and in truth, we experience the peace of God that keeps us steady in the storms of life.

A TALE OF TWO CHURCHES

If doctrine is a description of reality through which we make sense of our lives, then how you hold your doctrine matters. Churches tend to land somewhere on a spectrum between two poles. On one side of the pole is fundamentalism. On the other side is a non-anxious environment.

In terms of deconstruction, the crisis of faith is the anxiety someone experiences. A non-anxious environment is a church where its members aren't being drawn into unhealthy reactions to someone else's crisis of faith. By contrast, a fundamentalist church would see a crisis of faith as a threat and allow the individual's anxiety around their crisis to induce anxiety-filled reactions in trying to tamp down the crisis.

The opposite of fundamentalism isn't necessarily liberalism; it's a non-anxious environment. Which means that one way to define fundamentalism would be an anxious environment. A church can hold to conservative doctrine yet conduct themselves with peace in the face of someone's crisis. A liberal or progressive church can seem open and inclusive with their language but actually exude a significant amount of anxiety when someone questions their status quo, which would, ironically, make them fundamentalist.

Returning to Friedman's theory of anxiety, he describes anxious environments using five characteristics:

1. Reactivity: the vicious cycle of intense reactions of each member to one another

2. Herding: a process through which the forces of togetherness triumph over the forces for individuality and move everyone to adapt to the least mature members

3. Blame displacement: an emotional state in which members focus on forces that have victimized them rather than taking responsibility for their own being and destiny

4. A quick-fix mentality: a low threshold for pain that constantly seeks symptom relief rather than fundamental change

5. Lack of well-differentiated leadership: a failure of nerve that both stems from and contributes to the first four[7]

A fundamentalist church is an anxious environment that exhibits most or all of these characteristics to the degree that they gridlock the imaginations of their congregants (as discussed in chapter three).

If these two types of faith communities exist on a spectrum, then the intensity to which someone experiences their faith crisis is most often proportional to the level of anxiety in a faith community. This isn't necessarily a hard and fast rule. Everyone's stories are different; but it is a common pattern.

The more non-anxious someone's faith community is, the less intense their crisis will tend to be. The more fundamentalist it is, the more intense their crisis will tend to be. So how can we tell the difference between a non-anxious faith community and a fundamentalist faith community? There is at least one way, and it is the way in which they regard their doctrine.

A non-anxious environment. In a non-anxious environment, the faith community can clearly and healthily delineate the importance of different doctrines. Gavin Ortlund (who wrote the foreword to this book) has done tremendous work in helping lay out a vision of theological triage where certain doctrines are held tighter and in higher regard than others.

Ortlund divides doctrine into four categories:

1. First-rank doctrines are *essential* to the gospel.

2. Second-rank doctrines are *urgent* for the church (but not essential to the gospel).

3. Third-rank doctrines are *important* to Christian theology (but not essential to the gospel or necessarily urgent for the church).

4. Fourth-rank doctrines are *indifferent* (and are theologically unimportant).[8]

By being able to distinguish between different layers of doctrine and phases of growing in one's faith, a non-anxious environment can helpfully engage someone at every stage. At no point is someone a threat to the community.

In this framework, someone's faith is experienced with layers, depth, and dimension. Someone can question and change their mind on outer layers without ever calling the essentials into question. Those who are walking with them never need to worry if someone is in danger of losing their faith if they question something like the age of the earth. Even if someone does question the core doctrines of the faith, a non-anxious environment can see it as another step in growing in their faith. Instead of being threatened by someone drilling into the core of their faith, they see it as an opportunity for maturity.

A fundamentalist environment. Fundamentalism sees only two categories of doctrine: orthodoxy and unimportant. And most things get placed in the orthodoxy category. Fundamentalism flattens the theological horizon and when one piece is questioned, it's equivalent to the entire faith being questioned.

If all doctrines are equal, you can see why someone who questions a doctrine that's either important or even urgent can feel like they are losing their entire faith. Someone might think because they now have questions about the age of the earth or the millennium that everything they believed before is now in question. Questions about gifts of the Spirit inevitably lead to questions about the divinity of Jesus or the authority of Scripture because they were never distinguished in importance.

What could have just been someone discerning a biblical perspective on an issue or realizing they land with a different tradition than the one they grew up in turns into deconstructing absolutely everything. When something that's not core to the faith is knocked out from under them, it feels like their entire house has been engulfed in flames when really it was just some mold discovered in a wall that needed to be cleaned out. The experience of deconstruction then feels like a journey from orthodoxy to heresy when, instead, it could be a journey of drilling down to the core of our faith.

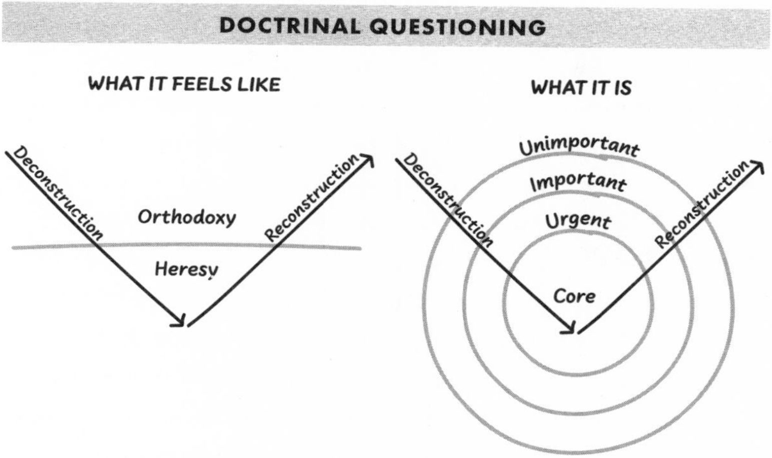

Figure 10.1. Doctrinal questioning in fundamentalist and non-anxious frameworks

I used to think that you couldn't hold a conviction unless you were 100 percent certain about it. I no longer believe that. I now believe that you only need to be more convinced of it than not in order to believe it, as long as you hold it in proportion to the level you are convinced of it.

I'm not equally convinced of every belief that I hold. I might feel 85 percent about one belief and 62 percent about another. There might be theological dichotomies that I feel 51 to 49 percent about, which means I'll hold the position but with the loosest possible grip that I can.

If you grew up in a rigid environment that only modeled 100 percent certainty about convictions, it's helpful to realize that you don't have to have complete certainty about every single belief that you hold. There are other options beyond total certainty and just giving up knowing anything at all. We might have heard about open-handed and closed-handed beliefs, but there is still a level of ambiguity about how to hold convictions, especially in the open hand.

Thinking in terms of doctrinal probabilities helps you gauge your level of conviction on a particular topic and engage with it appropriately. It allows you to hold space for mystery while still having convictions. It gives you space to either grow in confidence or change your mind down the line. It reduces the existential anxieties that come with needing to have it all figured out or pretending that you just don't care.

WHAT ABOUT HERESY?

Of course, while someone is exploring the core of their faith, it's almost inevitable that they will at least entertain, if not for a while *believe*, something that is heretical. A fundamentalist environment would simply see this as apostasy and disfellowship from the person. A non-anxious environment would understand this as part of the faith-building process and see it as an opportunity for discipleship.

I remember being in a room with two hundred other believers learning theology, and the teacher asked those who believed that Jesus was God's "first and greatest created being" to raise their hands. Nearly 50 percent of the room (of believers in a conservative church!) raised their hands. But that's Arianism! *Arianism* was condemned as heresy at the Council of Nicaea in AD 325. Were two hundred of the baptized believers in that room not *saved*? Or were they simply *mistaken*?

Most Christians who have been in church their whole lives might believe heresy or heterodoxy and not even know it because they have never been taught differently. The answer to someone veering into heresy isn't to make accusations or to immediately disfellowship. It's gentle, non-anxious discipleship.

If, after doing a deep exploration of the core of their faith, someone persists in their heresy and actively rejects the core truths of our faith, that is a different conversation to have. As we have seen, some people truly do forsake the faith. But the average Christian in the pews has never heard of Arius, Pelagian, Marcion, or Nestorius. Most have no idea about the heretical pits the church has had to avoid in the past, much less *why* they avoided them. It's understandable that those who don't know history are doomed to repeat it unless someone acts as a loving guide and helps them avoid the gutters on the right and the left.

WRESTLING WITH GOD

I have a friend, James, who planted a church in one of the most secular cities in America. He has found that most of the people who come through the doors of his church have deconstructed in the past, are currently deconstructing, or might deconstruct sometime in the near future. He told me the story of a young man who started going to his church and fell in love with the community. But when it came time to become a member of the church, he ran into a problem. So, James sat down to have a conversation with the man.

The man told James, "I've been coming to your church for a while and I love it. I love the people. I think you're a great pastor. But I don't think I can become a member. There's one problem. I'm a universalist and your church doesn't agree with me on that. It might be best if I go to the unitarian church down the street."

My friend thought for a minute and responded, "Okay, I guess you could do that. Let me ask you a question: Are you a universalist primarily because you have a high view of God's grace?"

"Yeah, that's exactly right!"

"Great, so, where do you think you'll experience God's grace more? In a place that accepts you because you believe all of the things they believe? Or a place that loves and accepts you regardless of what you believe? You might not be able to go through membership right now, but you can stay and be part of our community. Just know, you're loved regardless of what you choose to do."

The man sat back in his seat, "That makes too much sense, James."

"Why don't you stick around for a while and see how it goes?" James told him.

So, he did. Sure enough, it took nearly two years, but the man, while being loved by the community, wrestled through his beliefs and eventually became a member of my friend's church. Belonging came before belief. Sometimes, people simply need a non-anxious space to wrestle through their questions, entertain ideas, and give themselves permission not to have all the answers for a while before they find their way to the truth. My friend's non-anxious presence provided room for this man to disagree, take his time, and still be part of the community while he figured things out.

Ask yourself, if James had room for that man, did God? Was he a heretic, or was he at a temporary stop while honestly seeking God? Not all are blessed with the simple faith to accept God's truth the moment they hear it. Many of us, like Jacob, must painstakingly wrestle it to the ground, even getting injured in the process. But, like Jacob, we wake up from our wrestling and say, "Surely the LORD is in this place" (Genesis 28:16).

The beliefs we hold are more than intellectual answers to a heavenly test. They are the script of the story we will live out. They shape our imaginations and our character. They orient us toward God or away from him. That's why our beliefs and how we hold them matter. Not so we can be right, but so we can love the Lord our God with all our heart, soul, mind, and strength, and love our neighbor as ourselves.

11

RECONSTRUCTING DISCIPLESHIP

IF CULTURAL CHRISTIANITY and compromised churches gridlock our imagination about what it means to be a Christian, then reconstruction isn't merely a matter of intellect where we hold the correct doctrine. As we just saw, doctrine is important. But it's also a matter of our *imagination*. We have to ask ourselves: what picture of the Christian life are we holding up for those in our lives and pews? What sort of imagination are we, consciously or unconsciously, cultivating in others?

If doctrine helps us intellectually understand the true story of the world that God is telling, a renewed imagination of the Christian life—of discipleship—will help us understand how to *live* in that story. The life on offer in the Christian story is so much better than believing the right things and avoiding the wrong things until we die and go to heaven. It's an eternal adventure in God's good world. Re-imagining discipleship to Jesus starts with understanding what it means to be truly human, to allow God's design for humanity to become the vision that saturates our imaginations.

A NEW IMAGINATION

Every human person is a heart-soul-mind-strength complex designed for love. That is Andy Crouch's definition of what it means to be human in his book *The Life You're Looking For*.[1] That should sound familiar to every Christian because he's drawing that from the two greatest commandments that Jesus gave us: "The most important is Listen, Israel! The Lord our God, the Lord is one. Love the Lord your God with all your heart, with all your soul, with all your mind, and with all your strength. The second is, Love your neighbor as yourself. There is no other command greater than these" (Mark 12:29–31). The love that is contained in our individual heart-soul-mind-strength complex is designed to be channeled toward God and toward others. This is the center of life with Jesus.

As well-known as this passage is, for many raised in evangelicalism, this wasn't exactly the message we received, explicitly or implicitly. One of these aspects of our humanity might have been detached from the rest and held up on a pedestal of what it *actually* means to be a Christian. Maybe people are minds designed to know the right answers. Maybe they are strength machines designed for doing the right things. People could be hearts designed for feeling the right emotions. But it often didn't seem like people were complex, holistic individuals designed for *love*. As Crouch goes on to write, "To be a person is to be made for love. This is both the indelible fact of who we are and the great adventure of each of our lives."[2]

It's interesting that Crouch says that love is not only the indelible fact of who we are but that it is also the great *adventure* of each of our lives. As it turns out, the way you break out of imaginative gridlock so you can imagine new possibilities and expand your probability structures is not simply by learning more, but by reclaiming a sense of *adventure*. Returning to Edwin Friedman's concept of imaginative gridlock, he writes that the way to break free is by replacing certainty with adventure, embracing serendipity, and having the will to overcome imaginative barriers.[3]

These are the avenues that open our imaginations to new possibilities and, for our purposes, allow us to imagine a way of being Christian that is faithful to Jesus but free from the chains of a fundamentalist upbringing. But it's worth asking: Has our approach to discipleship done just the opposite? Have we made certainty the goal, delivered the answers without fostering discovery, and failed to give a vision so beautiful it stirs the human will toward wanting more of Christ?

We need different categories of discipleship that allow for the adventure of love. Categories that engage our whole being—heart, soul, mind, and strength—and aim our love toward God and others. These categories must allow room for people to grow, to discover God for themselves, to allow him to work in unique ways in their lives, and to foster their God-given creativity to love.

The three categories that I want to suggest are devotion, formation, and mission. Along with community, I believe recovering these categories of discipleship will allow us to grow in our love for God and neighbor for our entire lives, not needing to have all the answers and not needing our lives to be constantly up and to the right, but instead, seeking the face of God and the good of others with our whole being.

DEVOTION

Devotion might sound like an outdated word in the twenty-first century, but our devotion to Jesus as our Savior and king is where our faith—the knowledge of God's truths and our belief in those truths—and our hope for the future fulfillment of God's promises meet and mature into a wholehearted, existentially satisfying love for God. These three spiritual virtues—faith, hope, and love—are the three things that abide in the life of a Christian, and they work together to mutually reinforce one another.[4] For too long, cultural Christianity has preached a gospel where faith in Jesus means no more than intellectual assent to a few key ideas that save you from an eternity in hell. As we examined in chapter ten, our beliefs *do* matter. Faith in Jesus does, in fact, rescue us from hell and reward us with eternal life in the new creation. But if this is all there is to our faith, what else is needed once we have our get-out-of-hell-free card? Why should we give Jesus any more than that?

There is no salvation without knowledge of God and belief in those truths. Everything rests on what Jesus has done for us, not on what we do for him. We cannot sin our way out of salvation. And yet, there are times when our belief falters. We aren't entirely convinced of every truth all the time. In times of doubt and distress, we find ourselves like the man in Mark 9 who exclaimed to Jesus, "I do believe; help my unbelief!" In that moment, the man's belief wasn't strong, but he still acted as if Jesus had the power to heal his son, which of course, Jesus had. The man's intellectual faith was weak, but he existentially trusted Jesus enough to reach out to and trust in Jesus' power. This idea of *existential faith*—what theologians boil down to the word *trust*—is what I mean when I say devotion.

The problem is that what we mean by *faith* in the twenty-first century and what the writers of the New Testament meant by *faith*, while not mutually exclusive, are not the same. We're not wrong when we think of faith as belief, but our concept is incomplete. Faith isn't less than belief, but it is an *active* belief, not a passive belief. It's a kind of belief that moves beyond intellectual assent and into existential trust and practical obedience. It's a quality of belief that makes calling it a "belief" feel almost insulting. More than assent, it's *allegiance*. Allegiance is the active expression of our love for God that moves us deeper than knowledge or belief.[5]

You could substitute the phrase "put your faith in Christ" with "pledge your allegiance to King Jesus," and you would almost immediately have a more robust view of what the life of faith actually is. They mean the same thing, but too often our understanding of what it means to "put your faith in Christ" has been diluted to the point of being almost meaningless. It requires almost nothing of you. You can't pledge allegiance to someone *without* knowledge, but pledging your allegiance requires much *more* of you than mere knowledge. It requires your whole life. It's not just being right; it's being devoted. Entirely, wholeheartedly, existentially devoted to one man who is also God, Jesus Christ, the King of kings and Lord of lords.

I love how English hymnwriter Augustus Toplady spoke about this during a speech he gave in early 1776:

> When a citadel of the human heart is taken by grace, the enemy's colours are displaced; satan's usurped authority is superseded; the standard of the cross is erected on the walls; and the spiritual rebel takes the vow of willing allegiance to Christ, his rightful sovereign.[6]

Reframing it this way matters for all of us, but it matters for those of us who hit The Wall and experience deconstruction because it means that our faith is thicker than our intellect. It's more than the beliefs we hold, question, and reexamine. It means that we have pledged allegiance and existentially devoted ourselves to the king regardless of our level of certainty. We might have questions, but we're devoted. We might not feel his presence, but we're devoted. We might have been hurt by someone else, but we're devoted to Jesus. Our doubt and disillusionment are worked out in the covenant that Jesus has made with us and that we have made with Jesus. Our devotion is reciprocal. We aren't devoted to Jesus in hopes that our devotion will secure his love for us. We devote ourselves to him because he has devoted himself to us.

There's a reason the Bible depicts the relationship between Jesus and the church as a marriage between a bridegroom and a bride. As Christians, we're devoted to the bridegroom even if we're dissatisfied with the current state of the bride, because as the church, *we* are the bride, and Jesus remains devoted to us. Our feelings do not sway our faith, because we made a pledge at our baptism to be devoted to our king through thick and thin.

When our faith is understood as devotion to Jesus, it protects our faith from being devoted to other leaders, whether they be church leaders, political leaders, writers, or parents. Our devotion doesn't belong to them; it belongs to Jesus. We are only devoted to a leader insofar as they are loyal to Jesus.

Too often, faith falls apart when a Christian leader sins and fails. In those moments, the quality of our faith is tested. Was our faith in Jesus or in the pastor, parent, or politician? When we're devoted to Jesus, we want to see his bride healthy. That means committing to the church and holding it accountable for being faithful to the bridegroom. All human representatives of Jesus will fall short of his glory. Some will fail worse than others. But devotion to Jesus means holding fast to him and his people in the face of failure, not abandoning ship when things get tough.

Devotion to Jesus also provides an unshakable identity. Instead of being crushed by the responsibilities of self-belonging, trying to look deep inside ourselves and discover who we "truly are," we receive our identity from the Son of God, who is raised from the dead into glorious life. We can finally step off the treadmill of trying harder. There's no longer a need to achieve our sense of identity, worth, and belonging. We belong to Christ, our only hope in life and death.

Jesus transfers us from one story to another, from the story of the world to the story of God, "from the domain of darkness . . . into the kingdom of the Son he loves" (Colossians 1:13). There is no alternative story without an alternative king who is writing and ruling over the story. And we don't get to live in that story without our devotion to the king. If we're not devoted to the king and his story, we're devoted to the world and its story by default.

It's our devotion to Jesus that makes us take doctrine seriously, not the other way around. If you said you were devoted to someone but continually misunderstood them, misrepresented them, and had no desire to actually *know* them for who they are, then your devotion would rightly be called into question.

Fundamentalists want to make sure your doctrine is right before you approach Jesus. A renewed life of discipleship is devoted to the person, Jesus Christ, and out of that devotion, strives to think about him rightly so they can be formed into his likeness and represent him well to the world. Devotion to Christ is *faith seeking understanding.*

Our trust, loyalty, and devotion come first. The understanding will come later.

This is why it's of the utmost importance for us not to simply see faith as a one-and-done decision we made in the past but as an ongoing daily devotion to our pledge of allegiance to Jesus. When the storms of life come our way, the doubts of darkness creep in, and the cynicism of disillusionment overtakes us, it won't be our feelings or intellect that sustain our faith but our devotion to the king.

FORMATION

Dallas Willard famously wrote that the word *Christian* is used in the New Testament three times, while the word *disciple* is used two hundred and sixty-nine times. Being a Christian means more than merely taking on a religious identity; it's being a disciple—an apprentice—of Jesus. A disciple is simply one who responds to Jesus' call to follow him in their ordinary, everyday life. When Jesus beckons "Follow me," they drop their nets and follow him. But what does that actually look like? Willard gives us a fuller definition of a disciple:

> The disciple is one who, intent upon becoming Christ-like and so dwelling in *his* "faith and practice," systematically and progressively rearranges his affairs to that end. By these decisions and actions, even today, one enrolls in Christ's training, becomes his pupil or disciple. There is no other way.[7]

After we have devoted ourselves to Jesus, we don't stay as we are. Jesus won't let us. We begin to change the moment we devote ourselves to the king and his story. We begin to reorient our life around his life, our story around his story. We're united with him and begin to take on his character. This isn't a process that happens immediately. You can't *rush* it. You can *resist* it. But it's part and parcel of the plan. We are not simply meant to devote ourselves *to* the king; we are meant to become *like* the king. This is the process of *spiritual formation*.

Robert Mulholland defines spiritual formation as "the process of being formed in the image of Christ for the sake of others."[8] It sounds simple enough, but it's impossible for me to overstate the difference the category of spiritual formation has made in my faith. Once mired in wondering whether I was doing the right or wrong thing, whether I was being good or bad, whether I was "in God's will" or not, the category of spiritual formation came in and reoriented everything. It shifted the goal from trying hard to do the right things, to slowly and mindfully allowing myself to be shaped into the character of Christ by his Spirit.

Do you see the difference? It's the difference between getting the right answer on a test and learning to play your part in a story. It's the difference between a moment and a process, between law and grace. I don't have to beat myself up for not being farther along in the Christian life than I already am. I must only recognize that I still have ground to cover on my way to becoming more Christlike. Sin doesn't condemn me because Christ has justified me. Sin reveals to me the ways in which I haven't yet surrendered my will to Christ's will, and God's Spirit in me gives me the grace to do so. In this way, even awareness of my own sin becomes part of the process of becoming more like Christ. He redeems our sins for our ongoing salvation.[9]

Disciplines such as reading your Bible, praying, going to church, serving others, fasting, sabbath, solitude, and more, aren't laws to keep in order to earn God's favor; they are means of grace by which the Spirit slowly but surely works in our hearts to transform our character into that of Christ's. Spiritual formation is the result of our devotion being worked out in our lives over time. Through our habits, rituals, and the structures of our lives, we surrender ourselves to the king to become more like him. In *Confessions*, Augustine wrote, "It is a disease of the mind, which does not wholly rise to the heights where it is lifted by the truth, because it is weighed down by habit."[10] The spiritual disciplines aren't about earning God's favor; they're about reorienting the habits of our life to allow the truth of God's story to get into our bodies until living in the story becomes second nature.

This completely changes the goal of our faith. We're no longer trying to earn our place, trying to stay in, and hoping we don't get kicked out. We're taking one step at a time to become more and more like the beauty we behold in Jesus. Our failures along the way don't disqualify us. Our hope isn't in our performance but in Christ's faithfulness to transform us as we yield to him. His Spirit bears the fruit of love, joy, peace, patience, kindness, goodness, faithfulness, gentleness, and self-control in us as we continually devote ourselves to him and order our lives as citizens of his kingdom (see Galatians 5:22-23).

MISSION

If our devotion to Jesus aims our discipleship upward to God, and our formation into Christlikeness aims our discipleship inward to our hearts, then our participation in God's mission aims our discipleship outward to others. It infuses every single thing we do with divine significance. "So, whether you eat or drink, or whatever you do, do everything for the glory of God" (1 Corinthians 10:31). God's mission includes being a missionary overseas and evangelizing our neighbors. Still, contrary to what many were taught in more fundamentalist environments, it expands much farther than just those two things. It encompasses our entire lives.

I've never liked this common phrase in some evangelical circles: "bringing God's kingdom." That is far too big of a task for you or me as individuals, and it's not an idea you'll find in the Bible. It has much more in common with the "change the world" rhetoric that millennials had when we were more optimistic about the world, or Steve Jobs's "put a dent in the universe," than anything you'll find in the New Testament.

What you will find in the Bible is language about being "citizens of heaven" (Philippians 1:27), the church being a "holy nation" (1 Peter 2:9) and "the body of Christ" (1 Corinthians 12:27). Even Jesus himself said,

"The kingdom of God is not coming with something observable; no one will say, 'See here!' or 'There!' For you see, the kingdom of God is in your midst" (Luke 17:20-21). The kingdom of God is simultaneously coming sometime in the future and is already here in our midst. But even though the kingdom is coming, it's not something that we bring; it's an *inevitability*. It *is* coming and *will* come. Our role is not to *bring* the kingdom to earth, but to *pray* for God to bring his kingdom (Matthew 6:10) and *participate* in it as citizens of that future kingdom.

Being a citizen of God's kingdom in Christ makes us ambassadors of the king, who is making an appeal to the world to be reconciled to God (2 Corinthians 5:19-21). We are called to cultivate God's good world for the flourishing of all people (Genesis 1:28-31). God uses our work to provide for others and contribute to their good. He uses us in relationships to heal and speak life into the world, dignifying others in how we relate to them. Through our everyday, ordinary lives, we testify to the glory and goodness of God.

Tish Harrison Warren writes, "We are part of God's big vision and mission—the redemption of all things—through the earthy craft of living out our vocation, hour by hour, task by task. I want to do the big work of the kingdom, but I have to learn to live it out in the small tasks before me—the *missio Dei* in the daily grind."[11] The vocation of participating in God's mission to renew all things is core to being God's image bearer. We are God's representatives in the world, bearing his name with us everywhere we go.[12]

Everything we do matters in God's kingdom. Every job and every relationship are opportunities to love God and neighbor. Your dignity isn't greater or lesser depending on your paycheck. Everything that serves another person in love is valuable in the kingdom of God.

Our vocations are the vehicle that God uses to provide for the world. If you prepare food in a restaurant, God feeds the world through you. If you are a plumber, God provides water and removes waste and creates a livable habitat in his world through you. If you are a designer, God displays beauty through you. If you are a salesperson, God solves people's problems through you. You don't need a dream job to matter in the kingdom of God. God is making his appeal through you in the very spot that you are at right now with all the strength you lend to the world.

No other creed, confession, philosophy, or cause gives life as much purpose as the kingdom of God. Our discipleship to Jesus consists of following his way for the healing and restoration of the whole world. Nothing is wasted under the rule and reign of King Jesus. God cares about our whole life, and our whole life matters in God's kingdom.

As we are formed into the image of Christ, we develop godly wisdom for how to navigate the difficulties of life. We can respond to people and problems in ways that demonstrate God's love, grace, and peace instead of sinful selfishness, anger, or fear. Our ambition is redeemed and shaped into wise, godly ambition that seeks to serve others rather than ourselves. We reflect God to our neighbors when we embody his character in the places where we actually are, not in some theoretical doctrinal argument, but in the kingdom case study of our ordinary lives.

That's why it's so liberating to *receive* our purpose from God instead of *achieving* it all on our own. The kingdom of God is not a meritocracy where only the elite make it. Its doors are opened by grace. Our mission is to live as citizens of God's kingdom and give the world a taste of it here and now.

BEFORE THE FACE OF GOD

Far too many people who were raised in evangelicalism were told that this life was nothing more than a waiting period before they got to heaven. God felt far away, distant, and like he didn't care about their lives. But this couldn't be farther from the truth. This life in Christ is an adventure of living in the kingdom of God amid the kingdoms of the world. We all live our lives *coram Deo*, "before the face of God." He sees us, knows us, and cares for us. He is active in our lives, shaping us into his image, and forming our character into Christ's character.

He gives us meaning in our lives that frees us from the treadmill of trying harder and infuses our lives with a purpose that we could never find on our own.

The story we believe is the life that we will live. Finding our place in God's story, under his loving gaze, is the safest place we can be. Not because it protects us from all harm, but because our houses are built on the rock, and when the wind and waves come, we will not be shaken.

12

RECONSTRUCTING CHURCH

Our discipleship doesn't happen in a vacuum; it happens in the context of the local church. Story after story of deconstruction tells of the horrors people have experienced in the church. As we explored in chapter five, compromised churches have produced rot in people's faith that has to be rooted out. Is it possible to reconstruct our churches to have fertile soil for faith to take root, grow, and thrive? I believe it is. But how?

As hurt as I've been by church, I've also experienced healing in healthy churches. These churches were different, both relationally and structurally. I've been blessed to meet pastors across the country who minister in primarily post-Christian contexts and find that their churches are full of people who either have deconstructed or are deconstructing. These people are skeptical of church, don't trust institutions, and aren't entirely sure what they believe. But they find themselves drawn to these churches anyway. These churches give me hope that it's possible for the local church to foster meaningful community, help people heal from their wounds, and create a space for faith to flourish.

One of these pastors, Brad Edwards, pastor of The Table in Boulder, Colorado, shared a transformative story about a polyamorous atheist he met during the early days of his church. They began having spiritual conversations with each other, diving into Tim Keller's *The Reason for God*. Although the man initially felt the book didn't address his personal questions, he remained curious and continued attending church events.

As the church prepared for its official launch, an event the man wasn't specifically invited to, he felt compelled to meet with Brad and pray with him that night. As they talked together in Brad's home, in an unexpected moment, the man wholeheartedly embraced Jesus as his Lord. That night, the birthday that was intended for the church became this man's birthday for his new life in Christ.

Another pastor I've gotten to know is Nicholas McDonald, a pastor at Redeemer Church Indianapolis. He shared with me the story of Joseph, a young man wrestling with profound questions about God's sovereignty and the trustworthiness of the Bible. On joining Redeemer, Joseph didn't find answers to all his intellectual questions—though he did find some of them. Instead, he was introduced to a deep, embodied liturgy that resonated with his entire self—mind, body, and emotions. He came to understand that beneath his intellectual uncertainties lay emotional concerns, primarily questioning God's goodness based on his prior church's indifference toward the poor. For Joseph, the path to clarity wasn't through academic arguments. Instead, it was the consistent, immersive practices of worship, taking Communion, confessing sins, and receiving answers that truly addressed his doubts. He realized that to truly find peace, he needed to surrender his will, a transformation that was facilitated not by apologetics but by living his faith through liturgy.

Finally, there is the church where I'm a member. There are many things that drew me to our church, but one of them was observing the number of people in their late twenties and early thirties who had been at the church for more than ten years. There are many of them! How many churches do you know that have kept millennials around for more than ten years? When all around me people my age seem to be leaving the faith, our church is seeing young adults *keep* the faith. There is an obvious, concerted effort from my pastors to care for those under their watch. As one of our ministers, Roy, told me, "We have a relational staff. We care about people, and that's the most important thing to us."

DEVOTIONAL CHURCHES

Churches like The Table, Redeemer Church Indianapolis, and my church give me hope. Too many people have been hurt and abused by compromised, performative churches, and those are the stories that we tend to hear. We don't hear about the churches that aren't performative but are devoted to Christ as their king and their neighbor as someone to be loved. It's difficult to say which kind of church is the norm and which is the exception. But no matter which is which, we need more healthy churches and fewer performative churches.

If compromised churches are performative, then healthy churches are *devotional*—they are devoted to Christ and foster devotion to Christ in their congregations. I want to propose four categories that make up devotional churches that can help us think through how we can structure our churches to promote people's flourishing, whether that be before someone deconstructs their faith or while someone is deconstructing.

It might be helpful to think of these categories as four kinds of *spaces*. Those spaces are scriptural spaces, sacramental spaces, social spaces, and shepherding spaces. I believe that if our churches had all four of these spaces, we would be well on our way to de-platforming the performative churches and creating devotional churches that faithfully exalt Jesus as Lord and form people in his image.

These categories are an attempt to lean on the wisdom of pastors who have seen the Lord work in the lives of people who have been hurt by the church, and what has personally ministered to me. I include practical suggestions on how to reconstruct churches where people who are struggling with their faith don't feel the need to leave the church in order to work through their doubts and concerns.

However, it will take wisdom, discernment, and creativity to know how to implement these spaces in your congregation. All I ask is that you consider, with those who lead with you, what this would look like in your church.

And one more thing before we get into it: if you read this and feel overwhelmed by changes that need to be made or that this is another way for you to perform and succeed, this might be a good time to take a deep breath and release yourself from that pressure. The aim is not to find new ways to perform; it's to opt out of the performance altogether. None of this is new. In fact, these suggestions are old. We need more *retrieval* and less *innovation*. What I hope this does is simplify the church in ways that take pressure off pastors and congregants to be performers for each other so that they can behold the grace and goodness of Jesus.

Scriptural spaces. The first space we need in our churches is scriptural space. Scripture—not our ideas, personalities, visions, or innovations—is the standard for the church and Christian life. Everything we do as Christians is measured by the Bible and we submit to it as our final authority.[1]

But not only that, the Bible is one of the primary means through which the Holy Spirit ministers to us. "For the word of God is living and effective and sharper than any double-edged sword, penetrating as far as the separation of soul and spirit, joints and marrow. It is able to judge the thoughts and intentions of the heart" (Hebrews 4:12). Being exposed to the Word of God in Scripture exposes us to the God who inspired it. It exposes our thoughts and intentions before him, correcting us and penetrating our spirit. We do a disservice to people when we hide God's Word from them because, in doing so, we hide God himself from them. The Holy Spirit can work through the words of Scripture to cut through our doubts in ways that are beyond our ability and control.[2] "The word is the vehicle of God's power."[3] We need spaces in our church that expose us to God's Word in deep, meaningful ways.

As obvious as it might sound, the sermon on Sunday exposes people to God's Word. After my experience in different churches, I no longer take this for granted. Instead of being merely the pastor's thoughts, using Scripture to make their own point, devotional churches open up the Scriptures and bring out treasures new and old (Matthew 13:52). God's people need the whole Bible preached, not skipping over uncomfortable parts or only returning to familiar, comforting parts.

Not only that, but the public reading of Scripture has been the norm throughout church history. Members of the church can read passages throughout the service so people experience God's Word mediated to them by believers who are just like them in some ways and completely different from them in other ways. The effectiveness of God's Word is not dependent on the communication ability of the pastor. God's Word should comfort and convict, challenge and sustain us. It should lead us out of falsehood and into the truth, directing our worship away from idols and to God alone.

Bible studies are great ways to easily dive deeper into the Bible, studying it on your own and with others, gaining confidence and competence in reading God's Word and hearing his voice in it. I know this sounds obvious as well, but I have been involved in churches where Bible studies didn't exist. They were seen as "too religious" or were replaced with popular books or the pastor's sermons instead of *the Bible*.

The Bible might have primacy in these environments, but relational connections can happen here too. There is no one-size-fits-all way to get involved at a church, but I often wonder what would happen if one of the first things we encouraged new people to do to get involved at a church is to attend the weekly Bible study instead of immediately volunteering in a ministry, as is the practice in some churches. They would be exposed to God's Word and meet people to help them get more involved at the same time.

With the right culture, Bible studies are great places for people to wrestle through their doubts and questions too. Table leaders can be trained on how to handle tough questions with a non-anxious presence and be able to facilitate the conversation so someone is welcome with their doubts and feels safe to process them out loud without fear of being shamed or ostracized. Many churches have Bible studies already. There is nothing innovative about this suggestion. But with a little extra intentionality, it is a great environment for people to wrestle through their faith with God's Word and in community.

Midweek classes have all the same benefits that a Bible study does, but they can serve more specific purposes than what a Bible study can accomplish. This type of environment laid the foundation for me to reconstruct my faith. I joined a year-long theological training program that was essentially a seminary-level course in the context of a local church.[4] I learned the core doctrines of the faith, spiritual disciplines, church history, and the story of Scripture. I can't overstate how important this program was for my faith.

A unique opportunity that classes provide in the life of the church is not just the catechesis of your congregation but *counter*-catechesis. In his small but mighty book, *How to Reach the West Again*, Tim Keller argues that all catechesis is counter-catechesis:

> In our counter-catechesis, each of the basic narratives of the secular catechism will have to be identified, stated with examples from today's culture, affirmed in part because it usually represents a distortion or idolatrous imbalance of something true, subverted and critiqued, and shown to be fulfilled in its best form only in Christ.[5]

While this is possible to do in a sermon and Bible study, classes allow you more focused time, attention, and subject matter to do this well. Consider forming classes around the story of Scripture, the basics of Christian belief, spiritual disciplines, church history, cultural and practical issues, and more. This gives you the opportunity to counter our culture's false stories, apply the Bible's true story to real-life situations, allow people to work through their doubts and questions, and myth-bust any misinformation that someone might have picked up somewhere along the way.

Sacramental spaces. If Scripture is an encounter with God through his Word, the sacraments are an encounter with God through his body. In baptism, we enter his body, the church, through the sign of the covenant. In the Lord's Supper, we are spiritually nourished by his body that was broken and his blood that was spilled for us. In the sacraments, we don't just hear about God; we feel, see, touch, and taste him. All of our senses are engaged as we encounter the Lord.

There is something mysterious that happens in the sacraments. In baptism, we are washed clean and initiated into a new family, kingdom, and life. In the Lord's Supper, Jesus meets us, by his Spirit, and reminds us of his death on the cross while simultaneously pointing us forward to the future feast we will partake of in the new Jerusalem. We need signs and symbols, encounters and experiences that look ridiculous on the surface but are inexplicably meaningful deep in our souls.[6]

Many deconstruct Christianity and look for something mystical. They want to leave the raw intellectualism behind for something that feels real, rings true, and is rich in significance. The irony is that Christians have those resources right in the center of our faith. We don't need to choose between our minds and our hearts. The sacraments mediate a mysterious encounter with God by engaging our whole body in worship.

Many churches have moved the sacraments from the center to the side, sometimes only taking the Lord's Supper every few months or playing music with the lights down while someone gets baptized off to the side of the stage. I believe it's time to reverse course. Incorporating the Lord's Supper into the weekly service doesn't diminish its significance; it nourishes the faith of believers, especially of those who doubt. While their faith in Jesus might feel weak in the moment, they experience the strength of God's love for them as they receive a tangible expression of his grace through the body and the blood.

Baptism is the most important act of someone's life. The marking of their new birth, their transfer from the domain of darkness into the kingdom of God's beloved Son. Baptism isn't an individual act either. When someone is baptized, they are baptized into membership of the church. Their confession of faith in Christ is affirmed by those who witness the baptism and can help carry their faith through the troughs of life when their faith seems weak. Taking time to hear the testimony of a new believer God has saved as they're baptized edifies the church with their story and allows the new believer to celebrate with the people of God as they are welcomed into a new family. I wonder what testimonies of God's goodness we would hear from people if we highlighted baptism in our services.

While prayer isn't a sacrament, it also provides us with an encounter with God. Without prayer, we work in our own power—we're running on a treadmill instead of the green fields of God's grace. A healthy church is a praying church because, in prayer, every pastor, member, and visitor admits their complete reliance on God and seeks his face, crying out for mercy and aid.

As churches, we have a responsibility to teach people how to pray, facilitating moments where people can encounter God for themselves and allow the Spirit to minister directly to them. Consider holding a monthly prayer service. Whether early in the morning or before dinner in the evening, invite your church to pray together.

In many churches, prayer on Sundays has become a time of transition, allowing the band to get on or off the stage while the pastor gets ready to preach. But prayer is not a transition between scenes; it is an invitation for the Spirit to move and minister to the church. A dedicated time for the confession of sin and assurance of forgiveness helps people practice bringing their sins to the Lord and being assured that their sins are forgiven.

For those wrestling with their faith, this isn't just a time for them to be honest about their difficulties, but they also witness the rest of the church humbly bringing their burdens before the Lord as well.

For a few moments, the whole church is bringing their sin into the light and asking for forgiveness together. Even the person who is barely hanging on to their faith by a thread is not alone in their spiritual misery and need for God's mercy.

Liturgical prayers also facilitate communal prayer where the whole church prays together, confessing the same need, petitioning the same request, and lifting their voices to God as one. These prayers connect us with the saints beside us in the pews and the saints before us in history. There is something about praying a prayer that has been prayed by Christians for hundreds of years that connects you to the historical church, lifting you out of your present concerns and placing you in the larger story of God's people across time and space.

These prayers hold us when we don't know what to pray. Sometimes, we are at a loss of words, feeling unworthy or unable to come to God on our own. Liturgical prayers give us words when we have none, strength when we feel weak, and keep us communing with God even when it's difficult to do so.

Social spaces. The Christian life is unimaginable without the local church. It's impossible to live the Christian life alone. When we're born again into our new life in Christ, we're born into God's new family. In this new family, God is our father, the church is our mother, and we live out our new life in the Spirit among our real-life relationships with our new brothers and sisters.

In *The Great Dechurching*, dechurched casualties were twice as likely as other dechurched groups to cite "negative experiences you personally had in an evangelical church" as the reason they left the church. Many of these folks didn't feel as if they fit in or experienced love. Yet 17 percent of those who left said that they would be open to returning if the church was "a good community."[7]

As much as we need the church to connect us to God, we also need the church to connect us with others. Our life in Christ can only be lived out in real relationships with others. As a pastor friend of mine told me, "Simply being at church and having ordinary friendships is more effective than a dozen coffees with people."

In the church, we experience God's tangible grace through his family. We are encouraged in faith, held in grief, exhorted to do good works, and forgiven of our sins while we extend forgiveness to those who have sinned against us. "The church is the community of the gospel, a place for sinners and sufferers who acknowledge their need for Jesus and each other."[8]

You don't have to be best friends with everyone in your church to experience this. Every relationship, every connection, no matter how strong or loose, forms a relational web that can hold the weight of our sin, sorrow, and cynicism better than we can on our own. The church is an expression of God's grace in the life of the believer because, through it, he does not leave us alone. He gives us more than a weekly event to attend; he gives us a family.

One of the primary means of practically fostering community in the church is through what has been called *radically ordinary hospitality*. "God calls Christians to practice hospitality in order to build loving Christian communities, to build nightly table fellowship with fellow image bearers, to ease the pain of orphanhood, widowhood, and prison, to be qualified as elders in the church, and to be good and faithful stewards of what God has given to us in the person, work, example, obedience, and suffering of the Lord Jesus Christ."[9] Hospitality is how we welcome those both near and far from God to experience a foretaste of God's feast in the new creation.

Meals bring people together in ways that few other things can. In an age of atomized individualism and online outrage, it's difficult to be invited over to someone's home, eat the meal they have prepared for you, experience their gracious character, and walk away thinking they hate you because of your differences. God's people extend Jesus' free gift of grace to others the same way Jesus extended it to his disciples: through a meal. It's through the regular sharing of meals that relationships are formed, trust is built, and the gospel is proclaimed through the sweet aroma and delectable taste of a home-cooked meal. We would do well to encourage and equip our congregations to practice hospitality every chance we get.

Shepherding spaces. After our time at a particular church that ended in an incredible amount of hurt, my wife and I found ourselves at a small church plant that had just started with a pastor who, in many ways, was very different from my wife and I. But not long after we met him, one of his co-planters said something to me about this pastor that I have also never forgotten. "Here is what you need to know about our pastor: he is all in, every soul." And he was right. The pastor cared for every soul. If it weren't for this pastor, I'm not sure what our relationship with the church would be like today. I can tell you that I probably wouldn't be as optimistic as I am.

Pastors are shepherds, guiding and nurturing Christ's flock. As Harold Senkbeil aptly puts it, "That's what it means to be a servant of Christ. You get your hands dirty among his earthly—and earthy—people."[10] They should be deeply embedded within their congregation, not merely the face of a brand. The modern trend of the CEO pastor, which emphasizes organizational growth and efficiency, often overlooks the essence of pastoral care. Historically, pastors have been thought of as "spiritual physicians," emphasizing their role in addressing the spiritual ailments of their flock. Physicians heal; they don't exploit their patients.

The number one qualification for pastor isn't their skill, charisma, leadership ability, or relational skills; it's their character. Prioritizing the character of a pastor over everything else is the urgent ecclesial need of our day. Having witnessed scandals across every denomination, younger generations demand pastors who emulate Christ's character. While perfection isn't the expectation, striving for holiness and repentance when falling short is. But, in the end, it doesn't matter what a generation does or doesn't think. It matters what God has always thought. God has always required his shepherds to represent Christ in their ministry through their speech and conduct. "The work of the church is not the call to ministry. Our true work is that of manifesting likeness to Christ in all things, whether in success or failure, criticism or praise. If numbers, growth, and fame were God's measures, then Jesus would be deemed a failure. Likeness to Christ is not measured by such external things but by the extent to which a person's character bears fruit that resembles the fruit of the Spirit. Not by numbers but by kindness. Not by fame but by humility and self-control."[11]

THE CHURCH'S ONE FOUNDATION

Will this chapter fix everything in our churches? No. It won't. We cannot fix a single thing in our own power. We need God to move in our hearts and to seek him with all our might. My hope is that by reconstructing our ministries around Jesus, his Word, his people, and his Spirit, we will orient our hearts to God in ways that seem foreign in today's evangelical landscape and will unlock our imaginations toward a way of being Christian that seems all but forgotten in many places.

But while I'm overwhelmed and sad, I'm also hopeful—you might even say defiantly optimistic—about the future of the church. Why? Because Jesus promised that *he* would build his church, not us. All we can do is participate in his building project or get out of the way.

I'm not worried about the church's future. I'm worried about *our* future with the church. I want to be *with* God's people when Jesus brings his kingdom, not away from them. I want Jesus to come back for his bride and find a people who have been waiting expectantly for him, not seeking their own kingdom with other grooms who promised them power like Satan did when he tempted Jesus on the high mountain.

The church's one foundation is Jesus, not a pastor, priest, prophet, or politician. He is the only one who can keep his promises exactly as he made them. He alone is worthy of our devotion.

As the hymn goes,

The church's one foundation
is Jesus Christ, her Lord;
she is His new creation,
by water and the word.
From heav'n He came and sought her
to be His holy bride;
with His own blood He bought her,
and for her life He died.[12]

13

RECONSTRUCTING GOD

A. W. TOZER FAMOUSLY SAID, "What comes into our mind when we think about God is the most important thing about us."[1] Who we imagine God to be shapes the way we understand life and reality. A distorted view of God will create a distorted lens through which we view the world. Cultural Christianity, compromised churches, and our cumulative anxieties all work against us, obscuring our view of God and causing us to act and react against a picture of God that isn't true to life. A right view of God is like cleaning the window of our soul so we can see the beauty of God and his world in all its brilliance.[2] That means it's important for us to know God ourselves and help others know God as well, not just a caricature of God.

Coming to know God means becoming comfortable with all kinds of tension and paradoxes. For an infinite being who is categorically different from us, we should expect that God holds things together that we, in our limitedness, want to pull apart. Heresy happens when we try to relieve tensions; orthodoxy lives in the tension. Perhaps this is what God means when he says,

"For my thoughts are not your thoughts,
and your ways are not my ways."
This is the LORD's declaration.

"For as heaven is higher than earth,
  so my ways are higher than your ways,
  and my thoughts than your thoughts." (Isaiah 55:8-9)

I often hear this passage cited by people who are deconstructing as a kind of cop-out. There was a time in my life when I said the same thing. If there's something that we don't understand and even seems potentially abhorrent to us, well, God's ways are higher than ours; all we can do is trust him. Yet, there are things we *can* know.

It's interesting to me that many of the people who leave the church or their faith behind and go on to seek more mystery, mysticism, and intuition often scoff at this verse. The mystery of a transcendent God is at the very center of our faith. The simple confession that God is the Creator and we are his creation means that mystery is baked into the faith. For people who are deconstructing or who have left the faith to simultaneously embrace mystery and mysticism while being very clear—and rightly so—about things that go against God's design like racism, abuse, misogyny, and more reveals the first tension: there are things that we *can* know and things that we *can't* know.

DIFFERENT KINDS OF KNOWLEDGE

All of us have limited knowledge, but that does not mean all knowledge is inaccessible. I'm reminded of the Rumsfeldian Knowledge Matrix, which posits four kinds of knowledge:

1. Known knowns: the things that you know that you know.
2. Known unknowns: the things you know that you don't know.
3. Unknown knowns: these are things that other people know but you don't know or refuse to acknowledge.
4. Unknown unknowns: the things you don't know that you don't know.

Most of us live in peace with our known knowns. They provide us with a sense of safety and security because we know that we know them. "It's better to know than to not know," as some say.

God is full of unknown unknowns. We don't know what we don't know because he is so far beyond our comprehension that he truly is indescribable and uncontainable.

The middle two forms of knowledge are scarier. It's difficult to acknowledge our known unknowns because that means acknowledging our own limitations. "I don't know" is one of the scariest things that we can say, especially to questions that threaten our existential security.

But the worst of all might be unknown knowns, the things that other people know that we don't. Because far from acknowledging our limitations, this is where we must admit our ignorance. Maybe we're asking the wrong questions to begin with. Maybe we're heading in a direction that isn't taking us where we want to go. And maybe someone else can see it, but we can't. It takes humility to admit that other people know things we don't. That would mean that the reason we don't know it is because we haven't looked for it. And that would mean we have work ahead of us, to do what hasn't been done yet. Which means we really can't make up our minds until we seek and find out for ourselves. This ignorance, much more than our natural limitations or embracing the mystery of God, leaves us feeling vulnerable. Like an inside joke we aren't in on, we feel exposed and outcast from those who understand it.

THE OTHER UNKNOWNS

Much of fundamentalism is a reaction to these unknown knowns. The idea is that you increase your chances of staying faithful to God by keeping unwanted knowledge away from your children, church, or even yourself. This is where you have parents sheltering their children from Harry Potter, creating suspicion about other Christian denominations, or even casting judgment about all non-Christians being hedonic heathens devoid of good morals and common sense. It shouldn't be surprising that many people who are raised in these environments realize at a certain point that there is a world of knowns that are unknown to them, and they start to want to seek them out. "What were they hiding from me? Is it really that bad? I met someone who isn't like me, and they are amazing! What was all the fuss about?"

When they begin to discover things that others knew but they didn't know, they find themselves in a whole new world that is nowhere near as scary as they were told it was. As the saying goes, "knowledge is power," and for maybe the first time in their lives, now that they know, they finally feel empowered. This is why deconstructing fundamentalist environments is simultaneously terrifying and liberating. They're finally in on the joke, and it feels good.

But an issue quickly arises. They might have left their fundamentalist environment and have more knowledge than before—knowledge that gives them power—but they have only left *one* environment, one corner of Christianity. The reality is that Christianity is much bigger than any one tradition that someone is born into. It would take a remarkable amount of time and dedication to rummage through Christianity's intellectual history and make an informed decision to leave it all behind. Little is hidden from the annals of church history. There is still a whole world of unknown knowns yet to be discovered.

THE WAYS WE KNOW

While the four kinds of knowledge help us understand *what* we know and don't know, it doesn't account for the *ways* that we know. In our information age, too often, we assume that we can know all the things that we need to know simply by doing our own research. If we read the right books, listen to the right podcasts, watch the right videos, and search the right keywords, we can learn all that we need to know. When you consider that the amount of data in the world doubles every two years—and is on track to double every twelve hours—it makes sense why we would think this.[3] Even our access to information is fracturing and atomizing quicker than we can keep up. Yet humans are not simply information processing machines. There are other ways for us to learn.

There is a kind of knowledge that can only be learned relationally between one person and another. You can't know what your friend's relationship with their parents is like unless you ask them and they tell you. You'll never know what someone's deepest hopes and darkest fears are unless you spend years investing in the relationship, building trust, and being an intentional presence in their lives. We've been shaped to think that we can be information explorers, discovering all we need to know in the frontier of our minds. But the truth is that there are things we simply can't know unless another person discloses that knowledge to us.

Now if God, by definition, is infinitely beyond us, it makes sense that we could never discover all we need to know about him on our own. We're not going to study God like a new species on *National Geographic*. We need relational knowledge; knowledge we only have because he gave it to us. And in his grace and love for us, he did.

In Matthew 16, Jesus and Peter have a pivotal conversation:

> When Jesus came to the region of Caesarea Philippi, he asked his disciples, "Who do people say that the Son of Man is?" They replied, "Some say John the Baptist; others, Elijah; still others, Jeremiah or one of the prophets." "But you," he asked them, "who do you say that I am?" Simon Peter answered, "You are the Messiah, the Son of the living God." Jesus responded, "Blessed are you, Simon son of Jonah, because flesh and blood did not reveal this to you, but my Father in heaven." (Matthew 16:13-17)

This is the first time that Peter confesses Jesus to be Israel's Messiah. Notice *how* Jesus said Peter knew that he was the Messiah. He didn't reason his way there, nor did one of the other apostles drop a bombshell on Peter in a late-night conversation around a campfire. Jesus said this knowledge was *revealed* to him by God the Father. Through faith in Christ, we receive the true knowledge of God. Our understanding of Jesus' identity as the Messiah is a gift that was given to us by the Father through the Holy Spirit. How has he made himself known to us? In two primary ways: Jesus and the Scriptures.

HOW WE KNOW GOD

The writer of Hebrews opens by saying,

> Long ago God spoke to our ancestors by the prophets at different times and in different ways. In these last days, he has spoken to us by his Son. God has appointed him heir of all things and made the universe through him. The Son is the radiance of God's glory and the exact expression of his nature, sustaining all things by his powerful word. (Hebrews 1:1-3)

The apostle John famously refers to Jesus as "the Word." Jesus is the fullest revelation of who God is because he is God himself. It makes sense that Jesus would say the Father revealed Jesus' identity as the Messiah to Peter because the Father had sent Jesus to him, and now Peter was standing right there in front of him and had been walking with him for more than two years. He had been in a relationship with the walking, embodied revelation of God.

Notice what the writer of Hebrews doesn't say. He doesn't say, "In the past *we thought* God spoke to our ancestors through the prophets at many times and in various ways." He absolutely believes that God *did* speak to his ancestors. This is contrary to the popular idea in deconstruction circles that the Bible is simply "words about God" and not God's *actual* words.

Even Jesus held the Scriptures in the highest regard in his ministry, believing them to also be God's revelation. Contrary to our commonly held belief that the Pharisees held *too* closely to what we now call the Old Testament, Jesus rebuked them for not knowing the

Scriptures *enough*. Time and again Jesus asked them, "Have you not read?" (Matthew 12:3, 5; 19:4; 22:31).[4] He referred to the Psalms as "inspired by the Spirit" (Matthew 22:43), which is the same language Paul uses to refer to Scripture (2 Timothy 3:16), and Peter refers to Paul's writings as equal to the Old Testament Scriptures (2 Peter 3:14-16). The only way we know what Jesus said and did is because his apostles wrote what he said and did down for us. The early church received the words of the apostles as the Word of God (1 Thessalonians 2:13).

All of this brings us to a very simple yet foundational conclusion: *God can be known*. He can be known not because of our rigorous exploration and careful study but because he has broken the fourth wall, so to speak, entered his own story, and made himself known to us. The great mystery has been revealed and spoken to us, and we have been given the Spirit of God who searches the depths of God "so that we may understand what has been freely given to us by God" (1 Corinthians 2:12). We who are in Christ now have the mind of Christ (1 Corinthians 2:6-16). *We can know God.*

GOD IS . . .

If we can know God, then we can speak about God. As soon as we speak about God, we're doing theology. All other doctrines flow from the fountainhead of the doctrine of God. Who God is, what he does, and how he does it shape all other parts of our theology. Our view of reality is inseparably shaped by our view of God. Other books cover the attributes of God, but the project of this chapter is not to do a comprehensive overview of the doctrine of God—it's to reconstruct our vision of God from the crisis of our deconstruction. While there is much that has changed in my view of God from when I was deconstructing, I want to boil it down to three truths about God that proved to be the foundation of my reconstruction. God is *united*, *crucified*, and *alive*.

United. The single most foundational thing that we know about God can be found in the shape of our earliest creed, the Apostles' Creed. "I believe in God, the Father almighty, creator of heaven and earth. . . . I believe in Jesus Christ, his only Son, our Lord. . . . I believe in the Holy Spirit." Growing up, the closest we ever got to talking about the Trinity was eggs, water, three-leaf clovers, or just saying how much thinking about it gave us a headache before giving up. But far from being an afterthought, God being Trinity is the very core of God's identity, the foundational building block of who he is. As Michael Reeves writes in his book *Delighting in the Trinity,* "Because the Christian God is triune, the Trinity is the governing center of all Christian belief, the truth that shapes and beautifies all others. The Trinity is the cockpit of all Christian thinking."[5]

The simplest thing to be said about the triunity of God is found in the word "triune": God the Father, God the Son, and God the Holy Spirit are united with each other. They are three distinct persons, yet they are one essence. Of course, this sounds like just a basic definition of the Trinity, and it is, but tragically, we don't allow ourselves to dwell on the implications of God's unity. This simple fact alone opens doors for us into God's character that are all too often left closed.

Everything God does, the Trinity does *together.* When God acts, it is always *from* the Father, *through* the Son, and *by* the Holy Spirit. This is what theologians call the doctrine of inseparable operations. "Not confused, but undividable. They are who they are *together.* They always *are* together, and thus they always *work* together."[6] There is never a moment when God is divided.

What is true about God's essence as Trinity is also true about his attributes and character. God is not composed of parts with entirely distinct attributes that can be divided into neat categories. Certainly, we can look at the different aspects of God's character and learn from each one, but that isn't the *way* God acts. When God acts, he acts from all his attributes. This is called the doctrine of divine simplicity. It doesn't mean that God is simple to understand, but that God is simple in nature, not composed of complex parts. He is unified in his trinitarian essence and in his attributes. You can't pit different attributes of God against each other. "The Lord always acts in line with his entire character and whole being. In everything he does, God is loving, just, wise, holy, and good—infinitely so."[7]

This is true in all God does, from creation to new creation. Taken together, they provide a stunning picture of a God who is never in conflict with himself. God is always unified in his actions and character. Let's briefly examine one instance where this matters greatly: the atonement.

Unfortunately, in many of our gospel presentations, we talk about the gospel as if God is conflicted with himself. Father versus Son. Love versus wrath. It's normal to hear people who have deconstructed talk about the cross as "cosmic child abuse," where the Father murders his Son to save people from himself as if the Father were a raging, malevolent monster and the Son had to step in and stop the Father from doing something he'd regret. But this view of the atonement violates the trinitarian union.

The Father and the Son aren't against each other, working separately with different plans. God's wrath isn't separate from his love. God's wrath is not even its own proper attribute; it is always an expression of God's love. "God's wrath arises from his holy love in opposition to wickedness. Wrath only exists where sin exists."[8] On the cross, the Father and Son are carrying out the plan they have always had together to defeat Satan, sin, and death. The Father isn't punishing the Son, he is punishing *sin*, the very sin that the Son *willingly* took onto himself *for us* because he *loves us*.[9] As Jesus himself said, "No one has greater love than this: to lay down his life for his friends" (John 15:13). The atonement isn't an instance of God versus God. God is not conflicted with himself. God is united. And his unity is the very source of his love.

It's impossible to say God is love without saying God is Trinity. Think about it. Have you ever wondered what God was doing before creation? Before the planets and the stars, the land and the sea, the fish and the birds, and before humanity—what was God doing? Was he creating something else, something that we'll never know about? Was he simply waiting, sitting in the nothingness of precreation, biding his time until the perfect moment to begin creating? What was he doing?

This might sound like speculation, but Jesus gives us a glimpse into this mystery in his high priestly prayer. While Jesus is praying for his disciples, he says this little line: "Father, I want those you have given me to be with me where I am, so that they will see my glory, which you have given me because you loved me before the world's foundation" (John 17:24). Did you catch it? "You loved me before the world's foundation." Before the world began, before he created a molecule, before time and space, before the beginning, God was a Father loving his Son and a Son being loved by his Father.[10] That's the mystery at the center of reality.

This is the only reason we can confidently say that "God is love." How can you love unless you are loving another? And how can you *be* love unless you have *always* been loving? The doctrine of the Trinity is the foundation of our belief that God is, in his very essence, love.

This stands in stark contrast to other creation stories that surrounding cultures had in their day, and the ideas that we have about God now. Israel's rival, Babylon, had a creation myth that they wrote down in the *Enuma Elish*. In it, their god Marduk created humankind to be his slaves so he could stop working, sit back, and rest.[11] Needless to say, if that is your view of why God made humanity, then God certainly can't be said to be love.

If God is, as one writer says, "at least the natural forces that created and sustained the universe as experienced via a psychosocial model in human brains that naturally emerges from innate biases,"[12] then how can you make the claim that God is love? Love is something that we would superimpose onto God, not something that arises out of his very nature. If "God dwells within you, as you," as Elizabeth

Gilbert says in *Eat. Pray. Love.*, then God is nothing more than you loving yourself, which isn't love at all. Love must have a beloved that is separate from itself. If God is "a name for the transcendent within of every 'thing' in the universe" then God still can't be love for the opposite reason.[13] Love needs a personal lover who actually loves. If *everything* is God, then you can't sincerely say that God is love because *who* is doing the loving?

But because God is Trinity, he has always been a Father loving a Son. Love is intrinsic to his nature. Everything God does is loving because God *is* love. "The shape of the Father-Son relationship . . . begins a gracious cascade, like a waterfall of love, as the Father is the lover and the head of the Son, so the Son goes out to be the lover and the head of the church."[14] We are enveloped in God's love as we're united with his Son, by his Spirit, whom he has loved for all eternity.

Crucified. God is crucified. Even after the resurrection, Jesus still had holes in his hands and feet from where he hung on the cross (John 20:27). While this is easy to confess, it's difficult to allow our hearts to be transformed by it. When Paul is exhorting the Philippians to "have the mind of Christ," he turns their attention to Jesus humbling himself to the point of dying on a cross (Philippians 2:5-11). The cross is the power and wisdom of God on display (1 Corinthians 1:24) and is at the very heart of our faith. It's the embodiment of God's love. The gospel is the good news that Jesus has died on the cross for our sins. But that simple sentence raises so many questions. On the cross, Jesus takes away the sins of the world, sets captives free, and rules his kingdom from this throne.

Sin is our problem. Sin deceives and distorts us by exchanging the truth for lies, making us foolish while convincing us we're wise, and making creation the object of our worship instead of our Creator (Romans 1:22-23). The effects of sin can be seen in a close reading of Genesis 3, where we read about the fall. We see that sin twists God's word (v. 1, 3), deceptively appears to be nourishing and delightful

(v. 6), falsely promises to make us wise (v. 7), always affects others and is never merely personal (v. 8), causes shame (v. 7), and fear (v. 10), distances us from God (v. 10), turns us against each other (v. 12), makes life more difficult (v. 16-18), causes death (v. 18), and exiles us from God's presence (v. 24). Sin is constantly crouching at our door and seeking to devour us (Genesis 4:7). As Paul groans, "What a wretched man I am! Who will rescue me from this body of death?" (Romans 7:24). We all need saving from our sins.

Sin is the great equalizer. There is no one greater or lesser than another because we are all sinners. Unfortunately, sometimes this gets distorted into what some people call "worm theology," believing that because we're sinners, all humans are inherently worthless worms who don't deserve love. But that couldn't be farther from the truth. John 3:16 doesn't say that God so *hated* the world that he sent his only Son. It says that God so *loved* the world that he gave his only Son. God initiates his rescue mission because of his love for us, not because of his hatred for us.

Being sinners doesn't mean that we're incapable of doing good or even being virtuous people. It means that *every part of us* has been touched by sin. Maybe some parts more and other parts less, but there isn't a part of us that we can point to and say we're perfect. That's why none of us have any ground to stand on to judge someone else. We can't judge others by our own lives. Our lives are stained with sin just as theirs are. We live in bodies of death that need life. But we, who are dead, can't bring life to ourselves. We need someone to deal with our sin and death, take it on themselves, and do away with it so that we can be made alive. "Thanks be to God through Jesus Christ our Lord!" (Romans 7:25).

The cross is where Jesus deals with our sin by taking it on himself. It's the great exchange. "He made the one who did not know sin to be sin for us, so that in him we might become the righteousness of God" (2 Corinthians 5:21). On the cross, Jesus reverses the curse and gives us blessing instead. He takes the twisting of God's word and reveals it in himself; he brings joy and nourishment through his body and his blood; he is the wisdom of God revealed to us; he takes away our shame and shares with us his glory; he takes away our fear and calls us his friend; he knits us together in love; he gives us an easy yoke and a light burden; he gives us eternal life; and he draws us near to God forever. Jesus reverses the curse of sin in his own body *for us*. As Augustine wrote,

> Like men he was mortal: like God, he was just. And because the reward of the just is life and peace, he came so that by his own justness, which is in his union with God, he might make null the death of the wicked whom he justified, by choosing to share in their death. He was made known to holy men in ancient times, so that they might be saved through faith in his passion to come, just as we are saved through faith in the passion he suffered long ago. For as man, he is our Mediator; but as the Word of God, he is not an intermediary between God and man because he is equal with God, and God with God, and together with him one God.[15]

Jesus shows us that his kingdom is shaped like a cross. His crown is a crown of thorns, and his power is exercised through sacrifice. "God accomplished his mission of restoring creation through Jesus as he was enthroned as king on the cross. The kingdom of God comes in power, but the power of the gospel is Christ crucified."[16]

Alive. When God raised him from the dead, Jesus won the victory over Satan, sin, and death. He disarmed our great enemies till that day when he defeats them once and for all (Colossians 2:15; Revelation 20:14). Now, in his resurrected body, Christ is ruling and reigning over his kingdom from the right hand of the Father. He is our great high priest who, even now, while you read this book, is praying for you (Hebrews 4:14-16).

But his resurrection was only the first. "Christ has been raised from the dead, the firstfruits of those who have fallen asleep. For since death came through a man, the resurrection of the dead also comes through a man. For just as in Adam all die, so also in Christ all will be made alive" (1 Corinthians 15:20-22). Because Jesus rose from the dead, all who are in him will also rise from the dead. Every Christian can say, "Death has been swallowed up in victory. Where, death, is your victory? Where, death, is your sting?" (1 Corinthians 15:54-55).

We fail to understand the gravity of this because we don't take death seriously enough. We don't hold funerals anymore, we hold "celebration services." We don't mourn the sting of death and condemn death as an enemy to be defeated. We resign ourselves to it as the natural end of life. It's not. It's an intruder, a thief, a destroyer. You weren't meant to die, and neither was I. Death steals the precious gift of life that God intended for us. It's hard to explain the abomination of death unless you have been stung by it yourself.

Maybe that's why the stoics urged us to *memento mori*—remember our death. Moses wrote in Psalm 90:12, "Teach us to number our days carefully so that we may develop wisdom in our hearts." We rightly think of Christ's atonement in terms of the forgiveness of sins and the healing of our souls, but we don't think of it as the defeat of death often enough. Death puts everything else in perspective. This moment, this worry, this fear, this problem: What does it mean in light of death? Life is nothing more than a breath, here for a moment and gone the next. "For the fate of the children of Adam and the fate of animals is the same. As one dies, so dies the other; they all have the same breath. People have no advantage over animals since everything is futile" (Ecclesiastes 3:19). Everything loses its value in the face of death.

That is unless death is destroyed. If life really does go on, suddenly, the world is filled with color again. Things really *do* matter. Life has meaning and purpose and beauty and joy and love. Death becomes a passage, not an end. And the other side of the passage— the other side of *resurrection*—is more glorious than anything we can possibly imagine.

But it's not more glorious because we'll somehow be whisked out of this world and into an ethereal space filled with white light. No, we'll be raised in *our* bodies and in *this* world but renewed, animated by the Spirit of God. No more earthquakes and wildfires, tornadoes, climate change, death, and decay. Only life and joy that is sustained by the presence and glory of God.

The apostle John saw this vision:

> Then I heard a loud voice from the throne: Look, God's dwelling is with humanity, and he will live with them. They will be his peoples, and God himself will be with them and will be their God. He will wipe away every tear from their eyes. Death will be no more; grief, crying, and pain will be no more because the previous things have passed away. Then the one seated on the throne said, "Look, I am making everything new." (Revelation 21:3-5)

God isn't making *new things*. He is making *everything new*.[17]

The best part of all of this? It's all true. It happened. The resurrection of Jesus isn't a good idea that gives me feelings of hope. It's an historical event that happened in the first century just outside of Jerusalem. My faith isn't in ideas or feelings, leaders, or institutions. It's in one man who, on one ordinary Sunday morning, walked out of a grave that he was dead in for three days. If that didn't happen, game over. Call it off. Forget about all of this.

But if it did happen—if it's really true—the only appropriate response is to do whatever I can to organize my entire life around that reality. Because that means reality itself has been irreversibly altered. The universe isn't what I thought it was. God has entered in and drawn near to us. He made a way for me to draw near to him, and he's calling me to himself.

No matter what doubts, sins, and sufferings come our way, Jesus is inviting us to come to him. God is renewing the world, reconstructing the world that Satan, sin, and death deconstructed, rescuing us from the crisis that is our lives, and giving us everlasting peace. And if all of this is true, then like Peter in John 6, my only response, regardless of the obstacles life puts in my way, is, "Lord, to whom will we go? You have the words of eternal life. We have come to believe and know that you are the Holy One of God" (John 6:68-69).

CONCLUSION

C. S. LEWIS LOST HIS FAITH, at least for a while. After his wife passed away from cancer, he famously put his grief to ink in *A Grief Observed*. To this day, it might be the most honest look at the toll grief and loss have on someone's faith. You can be one of the most brilliant scholars of your century but lose your wife to cancer, and your confidence in God is shaken to the core. "Not that I am (I think) in much danger of ceasing to believe in God," Lewis wrote. "The real danger is coming to believe such dreadful things about him. The conclusion I dread is not 'So there's no God after all,' but 'So this is what God's really like. Deceive yourself no longer.'"[1]

The loss of God in pain and suffering is real. Our illusions of control are broken, our beliefs are tested, and we are forced to hold on for our dear lives when it seems like everything is falling apart, not knowing if it will hold our weight. Lewis says, "If my house was a house of cards, the sooner it was knocked down the better. And only suffering could do it."[2]

Deconstruction breaks down the walls that have been erected in our lives through all manner of sorts—culture, church hurt, abuse, questions, feeling out of place, and more. It doesn't allow us to stay comfortable. It's sink or swim, go all in or get out. As Lewis went on to write,

God has not been trying an experiment on my faith or love in order to find out their quality. He knew it already. It was I who didn't. In this trial He makes us occupy the dock, the witness box, and the bench all at once. He always knew that my temple was a house of cards. His only way of making me realize the fact was to knock it down.[3]

Sometimes, God has to test our faith in order to strengthen it. Not for him, but for us.

After a long, dark night, the sunrise is always the most beautiful part of the day. The sun breaks over the distant horizon, shining its beams over God's earth, illuminating the life that has been there the whole time. While deconstruction is a long, dark night, it gives us the opportunity to see God's light break over our doubts and disillusionment and shine in our lives, revealing things that were there the whole time that we never saw before. The darker and more harrowing the night, the more awe there is at the sight of morning's first light.

Even while we might feel the Lord's absence in deconstruction, he never truly leaves us alone. He is with us the whole time. In perhaps the most beautiful passage in *Confessions*, Augustine writes after his conversion,

I have learnt to love you late, Beauty at once so ancient and so new! I have learnt to love you late! You were within me, and I was in the world outside myself. I searched for you outside myself and, disfigured as I was, I fell upon the lovely things of your creation. You were with me, but I was not with you. The beautiful things of this world kept me far from you and yet, if they had not been in you, they would have had no being at all. You called me; you cried aloud to me; you broke my barrier of deafness. You shone upon me; your radiance enveloped me; you put my blindness to flight. You shed your fragrance about me; I drew breath and now I gasp for your sweet odour. I tasted you, and now I hunger and thirst for you. You touched me, and I am inflamed with love of your peace.[4]

So now we move forward in the messiness and brokenness of life. Casting our cares on the Lord, trusting in his goodness, and loving others as we have been loved by him. The Lord cares for his people, searches for those who are lost, and throws parties for them when they come home. His grace is infinitely wide, and his love is immeasurably deep. Nothing escapes God's notice, and he cares for every person. God isn't scared of deconstruction. He isn't scared of doubts or critiques, suffering or cynicism. He is the Lord God almighty, maker of heaven and earth, our rock and our fortress. With him, we will never be shaken.

NOTES

FOREWORD

[1]For more, see Jim Davis, Michael Graham, and Ryan Burge, *The Great Dechurching: Who's Leaving, Why Are They Going, and What Will It Take to Bring Them Back?* (Grand Rapids, MI: Zondervan, 2023).

INTRODUCTION

[1]Ian Harber, "'Progressive' Christianity: Even Shallower Than the Evangelical Faith I Left," The Gospel Coalition, March 7, 2020, www.thegospelcoalition .org/article/progressive-christianity-shallower-evangelical-faith-i-left.

[2]Little *o* orthodox. I'm still Protestant.

[3]Jim Davis, Michael Graham, and Ryan Burge, *The Great Dechurching: Who's Leaving, Why Are They Going, and What Will It Take to Bring Them Back?* (Grand Rapids, MI: Zondervan, 2023), 5.

[4]Davis, Graham, and Burge, *The Great Dechurching*, 24-25.

[5]Davis, Graham, and Burge, *The Great Dechurching*, 68-69.

[6]Davis, Graham, and Burge, *The Great Dechurching*, 75.

1. DEFINING DECONSTRUCTION

[1]David J. Gunkel, *Deconstruction*, MIT Press Essential Knowledge (Cambridge, MA: MIT Press, 2021), 23.

[2]Gunkle writes, "Deconstruction, then, is not a tool or instrument of investigation that is selected, taken up, and utilized by a (human) subject and applied to an object of knowledge. One does not, for instance, wake up in the morning, go to the office, and get to work deconstructing some object or another. Rather, the object of deconstruction is always and already in deconstruction such that the task of the human subject is to accompany or follow its particular unfoldings.

The subject, therefore, is subject(ed) to the object(ive) of deconstruction." *Deconstruction*, 28.

[3]Donald Miller is a notable exception. It's unclear where he is at in his faith these days since he has pivoted entirely out of writing about faith and into the business and marketing space.

[4]Stand to Reason presented this definition at their conference and shared it in a tweet. Stand to Reason (@STRtweets), "When it comes to 'deconstruction,' I have a question: What do you mean by that?" Twitter, September 23, 2022, 8:41 p.m., https://twitter.com/STRtweets/status/1573487714329952258?s=20&t=b9e8Qq2lj_vwLZAvKE2ugA.

[5]This has been expressed most succinctly by Lecrae in a tweet thread. See Lecrae (@lecrae), "A lot of Christians are afraid of 'Deconstruction,'" September 14, 2022, 9:31 a.m., https://twitter.com/lecrae/status/1570057592595963904?s=20&t=NaeqHJuj2v0tsGYg_TjVhQ.

[6]Rachel Joy Welcher expressed this sentiment in this tweet thread. Rachel Joy Welcher (@racheljwelcher), "Do not deconstruct without the Bible in hand, or apart from the local church," September 27, 2022, 1:54 p.m., https://twitter.com/racheljwelcher/status/1574835001572859904?s=20&t=d8ORCNXyZywm9lwHmzWrWA.

[7]The most common interpretation of these verses points toward the final judgment, and that is a fitting interpretation. Yet, it can also be said that we experience smaller-scale apocalypses throughout our lives that have the same effect.

[8]The formation of these categories was greatly helped by my friend Brad Edwards, pastor of The Table Church in Boulder, Colorado.

[9]Jean Twenge, *Generations: The Real Differences Between Gen Z, Millennials, Gen X, Boomers, and Silents—and What They Mean for America's Future* (New York: Atria Books, 2023), 248.

2. DECONSTRUCTING THE WALL

[1]C. S. Lewis, *The Screwtape Letters* (New York: HarperOne, 2001), 37.

[2]Lewis, *The Screwtape Letters*, 45.

[3]Janet O. Hagberg and Robert A. Guelich, *The Critical Journey: Stages in the Life of Faith* (Salem, WI: Sheffield Publishing Company, 2005), 94-95.

[4]Mike McHargue, *Finding God in the Waves: How I Lost My Faith and Found It Again Through Science* (New York: Convergent Books, 2016), 69-70.

[5]Richard J. Foster, *Prayer*, 10th anniv. ed. (New York: HarperCollins, 2002), 34-35.

3. DECONSTRUCTING THE CRISIS

[1]Elisabeth Kübler-Ross and David Kessler, *On Grief and Grieving: Finding the Meaning of Grief Through the Five Stages of Loss* (New York: Scribner, 2005), 7, Kindle.

[2]Kübler-Ross and Kessler, *On Grief and Grieving*, 18.

[3]Kübler-Ross and Kessler, *On Grief and Grieving*, 16.

[4]Kübler-Ross and Kessler, *On Grief and Grieving*, 15.

[5]Kübler-Ross and Kessler, *On Grief and Grieving*, 19-20.

[6]Lesslie Newbigin, *Proper Confidence: Faith, Doubt, and Certainty in Christian Discipleship* (Grand Rapids, MI: Eerdmans, 1995), 23-24.

4. DECONSTRUCTING BELIEF

[1]Michael Gungor, *The Crowd, the Critic, and the Muse: A Book for Creators* (n.p.: Woodsley Press, 2012), loc. 1660-1673, Kindle.

[2]Edwin H. Friedman, *A Failure of Nerve: Leadership in the Age of the Quick Fix* (New York: Church Publishing, 2017), 61.

[3]Christian Smith, *Soul Searching: The Religious and Spiritual Lives of American Teenagers* (Oxford: Oxford University Press, 2009), 162, Kindle.

5. DECONSTRUCTING CHURCH

[1]Yuval Levin, *A Time to Build: From Family and Community to Congress and the Campus, How Recommitting to Our Institutions Can Revive the American Dream* (New York: Basic Books, 2020), 22-23.

[2]A modified version of the definition from Jared C. Wilson. See Jared C. Wilson, *The Gospel-Driven Church* (Grand Rapids, MI: Zondervan, 2019), 25, Kindle.

[3]Wilson, *The Gospel-Driven Church*, 25.

[4]Jim Davis, Michael Graham, and Ryan Burge, *The Great Dechurching: Who's Leaving, Why They Are Going, and What Will Bring Them Back* (Grand Rapids, MI: Zondervan, 2023), 43.

[5]Davis, Graham, and Burge, *The Great Dechurching*, 46.

[6]Davis, Graham, and Burge, *The Great Dechurching*, 75.

[7]Diane Langberg, *Redeeming Power: Understanding Authority and Abuse in the Church* (Ada, MI: Brazos Press, 2020), 24-25, Kindle.

[8]Langberg, *Redeeming Power*, 7.

[9]Russell Moore, *Losing Our Religion: An Altar Call for Evangelical America* (New York: Sentinel, 2023), 33.

[10] Andrew Root's book *Churches and the Crisis of Decline: A Hopeful, Practical Ecclesiology for a Secular Age* (Grand Rapids, MI: Baker, 2022) is immensely helpful on this subject and expands on it further.

6. DECONSTRUCTING SELF

[1] John Mark Comer, *Live No Lies: Recognize and Resist the Three Enemies That Sabotage Your Peace* (Colorado Springs: Waterbrook Multnomah, 2021), xxiii.

[2] I got these three categories of sin from John Mark Comer, *Practicing the Way: Be with Jesus, Become like Him, Do as He Did* (Colorado Springs: Waterbrook, 2024), 90-91.

[3] Stephen Charnock, *The Existence and Attributes of God*, vol. 1 (Wheaton, IL: Crossway, 2022), 43.

[4] Augustine, *Confessions*, trans. R. S. Pine-Coffin (London: Penguin Books, 1961), 173.

[5] Joshua D. Chatraw, *Telling a Better Story: How to Talk About God in a Skeptical Age* (Grand Rapids, MI: Zondervan, 2020), 47, Kindle.

[6] Jean Twenge, *Generations: The Real Differences Between Gen Z, Millennials, Gen X, Boomers, and Silents—and What They Mean for America's Future* (New York: Atria Books, 2023), 300.

[7] Alan Noble, *You Are Not Your Own: Belonging to God in an Inhuman World* (Downers Grove, IL: InterVarsity Press, 2021), 35, Kindle.

[8] No hate to Taylor; I'm a Swiftie through and through. For the quote, see Hannah Dailey, "Taylor Swift's NYU Commencement Speech: Read the Full Transcript," Billboard, May 18, 2022, https://www.billboard.com/music/music-news/taylor-swift-nyu-commencement-speech-full-transcript-1235072824.

[9] Byung-Chul Han, *The Burnout Society* (Stanford, CA: Stanford University Press, 2015), 7.

[10] Noble, *You Are Not Your Own*, 73.

[11] Noble, *You Are Not Your Own*, 84.

[12] Noble, *You Are Not Your Own*, 94.

[13] Noble, *You Are Not Your Own*, 69.

[14] Noble, *You Are Not Your Own*, 77.

[15] "Our faith in the creative and even magical power of the self-fashioning self goes hand in hand with the decline in belief in an older model of reality: a God-created and God-ordered universe in which we all have specific, preordained parts to play—from peasants to bishops to kings—based on the roles into which

we are born." Tara Isabella Burton, *Self-Made: Creating Our Identities from Da Vinci to the Kardashians* (New York: PublicAffairs, 2023), 12-13, Kindle.

[16] Burton, *Self-Made*, 13.

[17] Burton, *Self-Made*, 14.

[18] Katy Waldman, "The Rise of Therapy-Speak: How a Language Got Off the Couch and into the World," *The New Yorker*, March 26, 2021, www.newyorker .com/culture/cultural-comment/the-rise-of-therapy-speak.

[19] "Is Therapy Speak . . . Gaslighting Us?," Wisecrack, April 24, 2023, https://www .youtube.com/watch?v=MBUEIwPKiak&ab_channel=Wisecrack.

[20] Jessica Lewis, "The Fight Over What's Real (and What's Not) on Dissociative Identity Disorder TikTok," *The Verge*, August 19, 2023, www.theverge.com /23823497/tiktok-dissociative-identity-disorder-doctors-backlash-diagnosis.

[21] Andy Crouch, *The Life We're Looking For: Reclaiming Relationship in a Technological World* (New York: Convergent Books, 2022), 142.

[22] Crouch, *The Life We're Looking For*, 139-41.

[23] Crouch, *The Life We're Looking For*, 139.

[24] Brad Edwards, "The Church Amongst the Counter Institutions," Mere Orthodoxy, April 1, 2021, https://mereorthodoxy.com/church-amongst-counter -institutions.

[25] Vivek H. Murthy, "Our Epidemic of Loneliness and Isolation," US Department of Health and Human Services, 2023, www.hhs.gov/sites/default/files/surgeon -general-social-connection-advisory.pdf, 4.

[26] Twenge, *Generations*, 302.

[27] Ronald Rolheiser, *The Holy Longing: The Search for a Christian Spirituality* (New York: Image, 2014), 99.

7. THE ENDS OF DECONSTRUCTION

[1] In my article for The Gospel Coalition, I wrote, "The goal of deconstruction should be greater faithfulness to Jesus, not mere self-discovery or signaling one's virtue." This view is also largely the view that A. J. Swoboda takes in his book *After Doubt*. That book is fantastic—I highly recommend it. I'm just wary of assigning a goal for deconstruction to someone who is in the middle of it. As you'll see in this chapter, I don't think that's the most helpful way of framing it anymore. It might be preferable, but it's not how I would talk about it today.

[2] Carey Nieuwhof, "CNLP 479: Philip Yancey on Growing Up in White, Racist, Paranoid Fundamentalism, Deconstructing His Faith, Reconstructing It, and a Message to Exvangelicals," February 28, 2022, https://careynieuwhof.com /episode479.

[3]Tim Keller, *Making Sense of God: Finding God in the Modern World* (London: Penguin Books, 2018), 34.

[4]Jenna Krajeski, "This Is Water," *The New Yorker*, September 19, 2008, www .newyorker.com/books/page-turner/this-is-water.

[5]Christopher Watkin, *Biblical Critical Theory: How the Bible's Unfolding Story Makes Sense of Modern Life and Culture* (Grand Rapids, MI: Zondervan, 2022), 11.

[6]Tara Isabella Burton, *Strange Rites: New Religions for a Godless World* (New York: PublicAffairs, 2020), 19.

[7]This number combines their subscribers between their *Rhett and Link* and *Ear Biscuits* channels.

[8]Rhett James McLaughlin and Charles Lincoln "Link" Neal III, "Link's Deconstruction—3 Years Later," *Ear Biscuits*, February 20, 2023, www.youtube.com /watch?v=RE_Iz-53ueA&ab_channel=EarBiscuits.

[9]Burton, *Strange Rites*, 28.

[10]Burton, *Strange Rites*, 31.

[11]Richard Rohr, *The Universal Christ: How a Forgotten Reality Can Change Everything We See, Hope For, and Believe* (New York: The Crown Publishing Group, 2019), 1, Kindle.

[12]Rohr, *The Universal Christ*, 19.

[13]Andrew Wilson, *Remaking the World: How 1776 Created the Post-Christian West* (Wheaton, IL: Crossway, 2023), 285.

[14]Mark Sayers, *Reappearing Church: The Hope for Renewal in the Rise of Our Post-Christian Culture* (Chicago: Moody Publishers, 2019), 33.

[15]Sayers, *Reappearing Church*, 45.

8. RECONSTRUCTING RELATIONSHIPS

[1]Augustine, *Confessions*, trans. R. S. Pine-Coffin (London: Penguin Books, 1961), 12, 59.

[2]Augustine, *Confessions*, 68.

[3]Augustine, *Confessions*, 69.

[4]Edwin H. Friedman, *A Failure of Nerve: Leadership in the Age of the Quick Fix* (New York: Church Publishing, 2017), 277.

[5]Jim Davis, Michael Graham, and Ryan Burge, *The Great Dechurching: Who's Leaving, Why They Are Going, and What Will Bring Them Back* (Grand Rapids, MI: Zondervan, 2023), 10

[6]Heather Holleman, *The Six Conversations: Pathways to Connecting in an Age of Isolation and Incivility* (Chicago: Moody Publishers, 2022), 24, Kindle.

[7]J. R. R. Tolkien, *The Lord of The Rings: The Fellowship of the Ring* (New York: William Morrow Paperbacks, 2012), 103.

[8]Augustine, *Confessions*, 111.

[9]Augustine, *Confessions*, 112.

[10]Davis, Graham, Burge, *The Great Dechurching*, 145.

9. RECONSTRUCTING SUFFERING

[1]Alan Noble, *On Getting Out of Bed: The Burden and Gift of Living* (Downers Grove, IL: InterVarsity Press, 2023), 103.

[2]Kyle Worley, pastor of Mosaic Church in Richardson, TX, said this in a class I was part of.

[3]Practicing the Way, "Practicing the Way of Jesus, Together, in Your City," https://practicingthewayarchives.org/practices/practicing-the-way.

[4]The Liturgists, "About Us," https://theliturgists.com/121-2.

[5]Elisabeth Elliot, *Suffering Is Never for Nothing* (Nashville, TN: B&H Publishing, 2019), 9.

[6]David Brooks, *The Second Mountain: The Quest for a Moral Life* (New York: Random House, 2020), 38.

[7]Ronald Rolheiser, *Sacred Fire* (New York: Image, 2014), 145-61.

[8]Augustine, *Confessions*, trans. R. S. Pine-Coffin (London: Penguin Books, 1961), 248.

[9]Timothy Keller, *Walking with God Through Pain and Suffering* (New York: Penguin Publishing Group, 2013), 314, Kindle.

10. RECONSTRUCTING BELIEF

[1]Ross D. Inman, *Christian Philosophy as a Way of Life* (Grand Rapids, MI: Baker Academic, 2023), 61.

[2]N. T. Wright, *The Day the Revolution Began: Reconsidering the Meaning of Jesus's Crucifixion* (San Francisco: HarperOne, 2016), 68.

[3]John Mark Comer, *Live No Lies: Recognize and Resist the Three Enemies That Sabotage Your Peace* (Colorado Springs: Waterbrook Multnomah, 2021), xxiii.

[4]I've seen this sentence attributed to Lesslie Newbigin, but I haven't been able to track down where it's from.

[5]Comer, *Live No Lies*, 88.

[6]Kevin Vanhoozer, *Faith Speaking Understanding: Performing the Drama of Doctrine* (Louisville, KY: Westminster John Knox Press, 2014), 45.

[7]Edwin H. Friedman, *A Failure of Nerve: Leadership in the Age of the Quick Fix* (New York: Church Publishing, 2017), 60.

[8]Gavin Ortlund, *Finding the Right Hills to Die On: The Case for Theological Triage* (Wheaton, IL: Crossway, 2020), 47, Kindle.

11. RECONSTRUCTING DISCIPLESHIP

[1]Andy Crouch, *The Life You're Looking For: Reclaiming Relationship in a Techno-logical World*, (Colorado Springs: Convergent Books, 2022), 33.

[2]Crouch, *The Life You're Looking For*, 30.

[3]Edwin H. Friedman, *A Failure of Nerve: Leadership in the Age of the Quick Fix* (New York: Church Publishing, 2017), 73.

[4]John M. Frame, *Concise Systematic Theology: An Introduction to Christian Belief* (Phillipsburg, NJ: P&R, 2023), 238-40.

[5]Frame, *Concise Systematic Theology*, 243.

[6]Augustus Toplady, "Let Your Moderation Be Known to All," in *Works*, 3:305; quoted in Andrew Wilson, *Remaking the World: How 1776 Created the Post-Christian West* (Wheaton, IL: Crossway, 2023), 247.

[7]Dallas Willard, *The Great Omission: Reclaiming Jesus's Essential Teachings on Discipleship* (New York: HarperCollins, 2009), 7.

[8]Robert Mulholland, *Invitation to a Journey: A Road Map for Spiritual Formation* (Downers Grove, IL: InterVarsity Press, 2016), 16.

[9]On this, Augustine wrote, "With awe in my heart I rejoice in your gifts, yet I grieve for my deficiencies, trusting that you will perfect your mercies in me until I reach the fullness of peace, which I shall enjoy with you in soul and body, when death is swallowed up in victory." *Confessions*, 234.

[10]Augustine, *Confessions*, 172.

[11]Tish Harrison Warren, *Liturgy of the Ordinary: Sacred Practices in Everyday Life* (Downers Grove, IL: InterVarsity Press, 2019), 95.

[12]"This is how creation was designed to function and flourish: under the stewardship of the image-bearers. Humans are called not just to keep certain moral standards in the present and to enjoy God's presence here and hereafter, but to celebrate, worship, procreate, and take responsibility within the rich, vivid developing life of creation. According to Genesis, this is what humans were made for." N. T. Wright, *The Day the Revolution Began: Reconsidering the Meaning of Jesus's Crucifixion* (San Francisco: HarperOne, 2016), 76-77.

12. RECONSTRUCTING CHURCH

[1]Harold L. Senkbeil, *The Care of Souls* (Bellingham, WA: Lexham Press, 2019), 37.

[2]Senkbeil, *The Care of Souls*, 41.

[3]Senkbeil, *The Care of Souls*, 43.

[4] If you're interested in learning specifics about this, check out J. T. English's book, *Deep Discipleship: How the Church Can Make Whole Disciples of Jesus* (Brentwood, TN: B&H Publishing, 2020), and the book he cowrote with Jen Wilkin, *You Are a Theologian: An Invitation to Know and Love God Well* (Brentwood, TN: B&H Publishing, 2020).

[5] Tim Keller, *How to Reach the West Again* (New York: Redeemer City to City, 2020), 40.

[6] Westminster Shorter Catechism Q 92: "What is a sacrament? A: A sacrament is a holy ordinance instituted by Christ; wherein, by sensible signs, Christ, and the benefits of the new covenant, are represented, sealed, and applied to believers."

[7] Jim Davis, Michael Graham, and Ryan Burge, *The Great Dechurching: Who's Leaving, Why They Are Going, and What Will Bring Them Back* (Grand Rapids, MI: Zondervan, 2023), 75-76.

[8] Jeremy Treat, *The Atonement: An Introduction* (Wheaton, IL: Crossway, 2023), 123.

[9] Rosaria Butterfield, *The Gospel Comes with a House Key* (Wheaton, IL: Crossway, 2018), 37.

[10] Senkbeil, *The Care of Souls*, 25.

[11] Diane Langberg, *Redeeming Power: Understanding Authority and Abuse in the Church* (Ada, MI: Brazos Press, 2020), 130, Kindle.

[12] S. J. Stone, "The Church's One Foundation Is Jesus Christ Her Lord," 1866.

13. RECONSTRUCTING GOD

[1] A. W. Tozer, *The Knowledge of the Holy* (Garland, TX: General Press, 2019), 1.

[2] Ross Inman, *Christian Philosophy as a Way of Life* (Grand Rapids, MI: Baker Academic, 2023), 141.

[3] Barry Libert and Megan Beck, "Leaders Need AI to Keep Pace with the Data Explosion," Forbes, March 26, 2019, https://www.forbes.com/sites/barrylibert/2019/03/26/leaders-need-ai-to-keep-pace-with-data/.

[4] Mark D. Thompson, *The Doctrine of Scripture: An Introduction* (Wheaton, IL: Crossway, 2022), 83, Kindle.

[5] Michael Reeves, *Delighting in the Trinity: An Introduction to the Christian Faith* (Downers Grove, IL: IVP Academic, 2012), 16.

[6] Reeves, *Delighting in the Trinity*, 34.

[7] Jeremy Treat, *The Atonement: An Introduction* (Wheaton, IL: Crossway, 2023), 107.

[8] Treat, *The Atonement*, 111

[9] Treat, *The Atonement*, 51.

[10] Reeves, *Delighting in the Trinity*, 21.

[11] Reeves, *Delighting in the Trinity*, 39.

[12] Mike McHargue, *Finding God in the Waves: How I Lost My Faith and Found It Again Through Science* (New York: Convergent Books, 2016), 255.

[13] Richard Rohr, *The Universal Christ: How a Forgotten Reality Can Change Everything We See, Hope For, and Believe* (New York: Crown, 2019), 5.

[14] Reeves, *Delighting in the Trinity*, 28.

[15] Augustine, *Confessions*, trans. R. S. Pine-Coffin (London: Penguin Books, 1961), 251.

[16] Jeremy Treat, *The Crucified King: Atonement and Kingdom in Biblical and Systematic Theology* (Grand Rapids, MI: Zondervan, 2014), 253.

[17] I got this turn of phrase from Tim Mackie at BibleProject.

CONCLUSION

[1] C. S. Lewis, *A Grief Observed* (New York: HarperCollins, 2015), 6-7.

[2] Lewis, *A Grief Observed*, 38.

[3] Lewis, *A Grief Observed*, 52.

[4] Augustine, *Confessions*, trans. R. S. Pine-Coffin (London: Penguin Books, 1961), 231-232.